the chef, the STORY & the dish

the chef, the STORY & the dish

BEHIND THE SCENES WITH AMERICA'S FAVORITE CHEFS

ROCHELLE BROWN
TEXT WITH ASHTON APPLEWHITE

PHOTOGRAPHS BY MICHEL ARNAUD

Foreword by Emeril Lagasse · Afterword by Charlie Trotter

stewart tabori & chang
new york

Special thanks to the following for graciously allowing their locations to be photographed: Ursus Books, NY (Daniel Boulud); The Museum of Modern Art, NY (Marcus Samuelsson); Kampong Tropical Botanical Garden, FL (Norman Van Aken); Manhattan Fruit Exchange, NY (Sara Moulton); Dan's Desserts, NY (Allan Vernon); Homestead Ranch, VA (Sam Choy)

Designed by Hotfoot Studio

Published in 2002 by
Stewart, Tabori & Chang
A Company of La Martinière Groupe
115 West 18th Street
New York, NY 10011

Export Sales to all countries except Canada,
France, and French-speaking Switzerland:
Thames and Hudson Ltd.
181A High Holborn
London WC1V 7QX
England

Canadian Distribution:
Canadian Manda Group
One Atlantic Avenue, Suite 105
Toronto, Ontario M6K 3E7
Canada

Library of Congress Cataloging-in-Publication Data

Brown, Rochelle
     The chef, the story & the dish / Rochelle Brown ; photographs by Michel Arnaud ;
   foreward by Emeril Lagasse
        p. cm.
     ISBN 1-58479-228-0
     1. Cooks--United States--Biography. 2. Cookery. I. Title

   TX649.A1 B76 2002
   641.5'092'273--dc21
   [B]
                                                             2002075828

Printed in Hong Kong

10 9 8 7 6 5 4 3 2 1

First Printing

To my angels up in heaven that watch over me everyday.
I miss them dearly, but I know they are proud of me.

My Great Grandmother, Margaret Wilson,
my Aunt, Joette Wilson,
my Pop-Pop, George Cooper,
and my Uncle Bobby

ACKNOWLEDGMENTS

First and foremost, I would like to thank my rock, my best friend, and biggest supporter, my husband, Marcus Johnson, whose love and confidence gave me the courage to write this book. My mother, Michelle McCeary, and my grandmother, Norma Cooper Wislon, have both always encouraged me to do anything I put my mind to—for this I thank you from the bottom of my heart with my deepest love. And my sister, Darchelle, for inspiring me to follow my dreams and for always being there for me—I love you and admire all of your talents. I also appreciate the support of my special dad and little sisters and brothers: Bruce, Eunene, Najaw, Alterek, and Ronald. And thanks to my special nephew Daquan, who is like a son to me.

To Emeril Lagasse and his wife Alden—you both mean the world to me and I cherish our friendship. Thanks to both of you, I am following my dreams. I am very lucky to have Emeril, Charlie Trotter, and Marcus Samuelsson as dear friends. You've all have taught me a thing or two about food, help me stay focused, and most importantly offer me your support. I appreciate everything that you do!

I would also like to acknowledge my new family that I adopted while working on this book. Leslie Stoker, President and Publisher of Stewart, Tabori & Chang, for believing in me, making me work really hard to bring this project to life, and giving me all your special attention and guidance; Jack Lamplough, Director of Marketing and Publicity, who is now my publicist, I thank you for listening as a friend and for putting me in the trust of STC. Thanks also to Ashton Applewhite, for your wonderful writing; Michel Arnaud, for bringing my vision to life through your brilliant photographs; Beth Huseman and Hannah Slagle for all your hard work and dedication to the book.

To all the chefs who jumped on board—Jimmy Bannos, Lidia Bastianich, Mario Batali, Rick Bayless, Daniel Boulud, Bernard Carmouche, Leah Chase, Sam Choy, Todd English, Bobby Flay, Matthew Kenney, Emeril Lagasse, Michael Lomonoco, Sara Moulton, Jorge Rodriguez, Marcus Samuelsson, Charlie Trotter, Anthony and Gail Uglesich, Norman Van Aken, and Allen Vernon—thank you for letting me tell your stories.

I would also like to thank my dear friends Lou and Terri Latilla, the best stylist in New York; Jaqueline Wilson, Sonia Armstead, Johnathon Johnson, Kyle Coleman, Jacqueline and Clarice Joynes; Karen Katz and Daniel Shklair; Donna Hanover, who has been my mentor; my college buddies Camille Bey, Dana Vernon, Kate Sexton, Myra Hardy, Erica Gainer, and Nime La Fauci; Pam Arnone, my make-up artist, and O'Neal Whyte, my hair stylist; Judy Girad, Susan Stockton, and my Food Network family; my family at the William Morris Agency, Alan Kanof, Linda Davis, Scott Lonker, and John Rosen. Finally, I thank Ricki Stofsky and Doris Weisberg my two adopted moms who continue to support and nurture me.

CONTENTS

FOREWORD BY EMERIL LAGASSE..............9

INTRODUCTION..............10

Charlie Trotter..............16
Cold Curried-Cucumber Soup........19

Emeril Lagasse..............20
Alden's Kicked-Up Cornbread........23

Lidia Bastianich..............24
Chicken Bites with Potatoes, Sausages, and Vinegar........27

Daniel Boulud..............28
Saffron-Flavored Mussel Velouté with Gratin of Mussels........31

Marcus Samuelsson..............32
Tandoori-Smoked Salmon with Citrus Salsa........35

Rick Bayless..............36
Mesquite-Smoked Grilled Turkey with Red Chile-Adobo Sauce and Jicama-Cranberry Relish........38

Norman Van Aken..............40
Chocolate Gooey Cake........43

Sara Moulton..............44
Soft-Shell Crabs with Spicy Tartar Sauce........47

Matthew Kenney..............48
Roasted Lamb Loin Stuffed with Almonds, Dates, Goat Cheese, and Mint........51

Leah Chase..............53
Green Tomato Casserole........55

Todd English..............56
Bay Scallops with Hazelnuts and Oranges........59

Bobby Flay..............60
Beet and Goat Cheese Empanadas with Orange-Paprika Vinaigrette........63

Bernard Carmouche..............64
Sautéed Rainbow Trout........67

Allan Vernon..............68
Vernon's Jerk Baby Back Ribs........71

Michael Lomonaco..............72
Pan-Roasted Foie Gras with White Peach–Chile Relish........75

Mario Batali..............76
Neapolitan Ravioli........79

Jimmy Bannos..............80
Chicken-and-Shrimp Orzoffee........83

Jorge Rodriguez..............84
Traveling Squab with Cabbage........87

Gail and Anthony Uglesich..............88
Shrimp Uggie........91

Sam Choy..............92
South Pacific Lobster and Seafood Salad with Honey-and Macadamia Nut–Crusted Banana........95

AFTERWORD BY CHARLIE TROTTER..............97

Q & A: THE CHEFS TALK BACK..............98

WHERE TO FIND THEM..............108

FOREWORD

About nine years ago, Reid Land Productions based in Nashville, Tennessee, approached me about appearing on a new cable television channel called the Food Network. At that point, they really didn't have a studio, but they were looking for shows and talent to launch this huge project. I began to imagine the possibilities that a twenty-four-hour channel about food would create—wine and food news, in fact, anything you could dream about related to food. So I decided to give it a shot and filmed a pilot.

The Food Network called me shortly after that to shoot sixty-five episodes for a show called "How to Boil Water." Then I met the creator of this channel, Reese Schonfeld, (who also pioneered CNN) and the start-up New York City team of around ten people, all of whom were working out of a one-bedroom apartment on Manhattan's West Side. One person from those early days stands out in my mind—Rochelle Brown. She had a glow about her and a determination not only to be in television, but also to be around food.

When the network launched with a full studio in New York City, I often ran into Rochelle when I came up from New Orleans for creative meetings or to film "Essence of Emeril." At the time she was a production assistant, and later became associate producer for a show called "Food News and Views." She was always eager to learn and her determination coupled with street smarts and that amazing smile were beginning to set her in a class of her own.

She started to make a name for herself, not only at the network, but throughout New York City. Her hard work, trust, honesty, and "tell it like it is" attitude were why people were taking to her. Even though we didn't work directly with each other, we began to form a true bond. Her loyalty, creativity, and professionalism impressed me and I became a real fan of hers.

After several runs of "Essence of Emeril" I was considering retiring from television, but I dreamed of doing another show featuring food with music, a live audience, and a lot of fun. One day I mentioned my idea to Rochelle on a whim and she said, "Emeril, go for it! You can do it." To my surprise it did happen. "Emeril Live!" was born, and not only did I get Karen Katz as executive producer, but Rochelle Brown as the producer. Wow! What a team.

Rochelle has become like a sister to me, but she is also special to the many people she has touched and changed with her knowledge, her passion, and her affection for people—not to mention her hard work. She never misses a beat, and her enthusiasm for both television and food is unprecedented. I can't think of a better person to unite all of us for this book.

My hat is off to my dear friend and respected colleague, Rochelle Brown.

Emeril Lagasse

INTRODUCTION

I was a kid who ate at Sizzler. My grandparents would pick us up every other Friday night and we'd head for Sizzler's enormous salad bar, or to the local Chinese restaurant, where I loved the red leather seats and dipping my fried noodles in duck sauce. My family was very close-knit, and every holiday—Christmas, New Year's Day, Easter, and Thanksgiving—we ate home-cooked meals that included baked and fried chicken, meatloaf, my grandma's famous twelve-cheese macaroni, rice and gravy, cabbage, collard greens, potato salad, corn-bread, mashed potatoes, and sweet potato pie. My mother and grandmothers were great cooks, and my pop-pop made the best coconut cake, but it was main-stream cooking. Food just wasn't a big deal, except to my Aunt Joette, who frequented great mom-and-pop places as well as fancy eateries. At the time I thought she ate out too much, but I realize now that she was the first foodie in the family. I remember wanting to sink under the table when she'd send a dirty fork back to the kitchen, or instruct the

waiter that her steak should be served medium rare, or tell the manager that her salmon had been overcooked and was dry. She was the first person to teach me about getting the most out of a dining experience.

I attended Douglas College, the largest all-women's college in the United States, at Rutgers University. Although I'd planned to be a computer scientist, after taking just one math class, I switched my major to journalism and mass media because I was good at com-municating and organizing people. In addition, I decided to add a second major in Africana Studies because I wanted to learn more about my people and my history.

Fortunately Rutgers offered some great internships in television. My first was at Suburban Cable in Piscataway, New Jersey, where I did a lot of coffee-making and schlepping, but I also learned about people and television. Because television is of the moment, every-body wants it and they want it now. The internship taught me how to juggle, which was extremely valu-able because if you're not versatile and can't deal with pressure and people's expectations, you're not going to get anywhere in television. As a producer, I have to keep a cool head, be able to delegate, make it happen. In any given day I could be juggling twenty jobs in one minute—the lighting isn't right, the food isn't ready, the talent isn't happy—and I have to put all those fires out fast because every minute is expensive.

After graduation, a human resources recruiter told me about an opening for a trainee on a morning show on the Fox Network called "Good Day New York." The pay was terrible, about five dollars an hour, but I was delighted to have the opportunity to break into the New York market. The job meant getting up at two in the morning in order to be at the studio at three to prep for a show that came on at 5 A.M. It was like having to get out of bed with the worst flu imaginable, so tired your body hurts. I had to go to bed at 8 P.M., and it made me mad that my friends had such great social lives and high salaries. But I knew I had to pay my dues and that the people I was working

for had put their time in too.

I got coffee, walked the anchor's dog, picked the red M&Ms out of the jar for the guest who didn't like red, and even ironed clothes. I was lucky enough to learn from some of the most talented and seasoned producers and executive producers in the business. They were fast on their feet; they never took no for an answer; they always got the story (by any means necessary); and they had the contacts. After nine years in the business, my own Rolodex now resembles a small safe. A good producer is a leader, too, and I've learned to follow my instincts and take the initiative to make great stories happen.

One day, after I'd been at Fox for about three months, a senior producer named Rickie Stofsky said, "You're the new trainee—can you cut these three pieces? I have fifteen minutes." Luckily I'd gotten a lot of hands-on experience at the cable station, so I said, "Tell me exactly what you want," walked into the edit room, and came back in ten minutes with the three promo edits. Ricki watched the tape and said, "Damn, you're

good." She was one of the first people I hit it off with, but as luck would have it, it was her last week there. She told me she was leaving to start something called the Food Network. It sounded ridiculous and we chuckled, but she said, "Everybody is giving me their résumé. Call me after six months."

I asked for her home address, went home, and said to myself, "I can't keep getting up at 2 A.M." I put together a gift basket with some wine and cheese, attached my résumé in the form of a menu, and included a note that said, "Boy would I like to take a bite out of this job." I had it delivered to her house, and she hired me the next day.

When I showed up at the midtown office, I was puzzled by the fact that it looked a whole lot more like an apartment building than a television station. As Rickie opened the door, I saw seven people working out of cardboard boxes in a one-bedroom apartment and I thought, "This is what I left 'Good Day New York' for?" There wasn't even a desk, not to mention a kitchen. Reese Schonfeld, the brainchild behind CNN, worked out of the bedroom. However, his latest venture, the Food Network, would soon become America's fastest-growing cable network.

I started as a production assistant working the phones, looking for talent, typing letters, researching, getting coffee and lunch, scheduling appointments with backers. I called on chefs, cookbook authors, food writers, and celebrities to pitch them ideas for segments and possible shows. They'd say, "A what? Are you kidding me?" I got an unusually large amount of responsibility because we were a start-up working on a shoestring, and we all did whatever it took to keep the network moving forward. I quickly went from second-guessing this career move to talking about the Food Network with the fervor of an ambitious aide spreading the word about an exciting political candidate. I was proud to be a part of this new venture and eager to follow all of Reese's leads. About two months after I showed up, we moved to our first studio space at 34th Street and the West Side

Highway, staffed by a whole team of producers and food writers. It was there that we started to shoot our first show. Because Reese was a newshound, it was a news show called "Food News and Views," hosted by Donna Hanover and David Rosengarten.

Four months later, Ricki came to me and said, "Hey, there's a housewares trade show in Chicago in a week and we have no one else to send, so we're sending you." I was supposed to come back with three packages, or sound bites, for the news show, including an interview with Julia Child. It was my true introduction to the food world, because at these shows cookware manufacturers hire all the top chefs to demonstrate their products. I arrived at the All Clad booth, and there was Julia Child with a line about fifty people long of news crews waiting to interview her. Another chef named Lidia Bastianich was cooking nearby, so I introduced myself, gave her the whole spiel, and she said, "Let me introduce you to my good friend Julia." We walked over and Lidia said, "You're not going to believe

this, Julia. They're starting up this network, like MTV or the Movie Channel, but completely devoted to food and food trends." A big smile spread across Julia's face and she said, "How brilliant! I think this is a wonderful idea!" I gave my cameraman the wink and Julia gave the Food Network her blessing.

At the show I met a man named Alan Lowenfeld. He was marketing a product called the Extendafork for tasting dishes across the table, and he invited me to dinner at a place called Charlie Trotter's. To me it could have been Charlie's Steakhouse, and I was a heartbeat away from turning him down. Since I didn't know to wear comfortable shoes to a trade show, when 6 P.M. rolled around I really wanted to put my feet up, but luckily, I rallied and accepted his offer. I got a hint of what awaited me when the bellman commented, "Nice place!" It was nice, a beautiful brownstone in Lincoln Park, on the outskirts of the city. The maître d' came right up and said, "Follow me to your table, Miss Brown. Alan is already here." I had no idea where he was leading me, but when we passed through the elegant dining room into the fluorescent lights, I realized I was going to be dining in the kitchen. There sat Alan and his guests at what I was to learn was the Holy Grail for serious foodies: Charlie's Kitchen Table!

I didn't realize it at the time, but the chef's table is the best seat in the house, the calm at the center of a storm of remarkable cooking. I'd been invited so all these prestigious food writers and foodies could grill me about the Food Network, which was fine with me because I was there to start the buzz. Sitting at Charlie's exclusive table was like being vaulted to the top of the food chain, and I had to act like I knew what I was doing. My idea of great service was a waitress who was courteous and brought you a prompt refill on your Coke. Here, the service was all choreographed. Each waiter had one person to attend to and they served you in unison, explaining each dish. The experience expanded my horizons, and I thought, "Average consumers like me don't know about this, and the Food Network is going to open

this world to them. This thing is really going to work." Most people eat for nourishment, but I was bitten by the bug. Food is about love, and for some people there is no greater pleasure than preparing food at home or in a restaurant. And then there are people like me who enjoy eating other people's culinary creations.

The Food Network started in 1993, just as the whole celebrity chef phenomenon was beginning. Julia was always Julia, but all of a sudden you started seeing chefs' names everywhere. Wolfgang Puck was doing the Emmys, and people went from wanting to know what Julia Roberts was wearing to what she was eating. The Food Network spread the message that it was acceptable, even cool, to have cooking be your skill and to reach people through food. As this culture shift started taking place, more and more chefs came forward from the kitchen into the spotlight.

Nothing brings me more pleasure than discovering people and stories, and I've always managed to return from my travels with new friends. I can get people to open

up as if the camera weren't there, so their true personalities and priorities emerge. As I started meeting these gifted chefs, I would make it my business to find out the secret ingredients of their lives and successes. Each chef had great stories about hiring staff, opening their first places, and living out their dreams of cooking their cuisines. Some I taught about television; others would share conversations about the culinary industry; most became friends; and all of them taught me a thing or two about food. That girl who went to Sizzler now spends her time among some of most talented chefs in the world. Food has really become my life, and I've become a foodie: someone who takes food seriously, doesn't mind sharing her food passions, and understands the food world—the chefs, the writers, and the whole culture.

On remote location shoots people often comment that they like working with me because I understand that they still have a restaurant to run, even though they want to do the show. I'm not going to interrupt that flow, because I understand what these chefs have to do in order to prepare extraordinary food day in and day out. In any given day, my job as a producer is to make sure all the elements of the show are in place—from copies of the guest's new cookbook to fresh tarragon to making sure the bar guests are the right fit for the show. Before each segment of each show tapes I check with the entire crew: the kitchen staff, camera crew, stage manager, production staff, and sound engineers. The audience is a big part of "Emeril Live!"; we have around almost two hundred audience members at every show, and we usually do about one hundred shows a season. I select and strategically place enthusiastic audience members, and also soothe the one or two unhappy people who invariably crop up. If a problem arises, I iron it out behind the scenes or during commercial interruptions, whether it means tucking in a shirttail or pumping up the audience. A good producer learns to roll with the punches and not get stressed out.

On a show like this, the producer is the liaison between the talent (the on-air host), and the guests, if any, and the subject itself. I work with our executive producer, production staff, and Emeril's home-base office to make sure the entire show is interesting and accessible for a general audience. Emeril, the production staff, and I go over each of the show's components in advance: the band, the breaks, the guests. A big part of my job is also to find guests for our show who are experts on different subjects and who have great food stories. They range from four-star chefs to butchers and purveyors to Dean, "the human grilling machine" who mans a twenty-five-foot top-of-the-line portable grill. Usually I go out and produce a two- to four-minute taped package with these guests—more if the show calls for it—and then invite them to be our guests in the studio. I explain what we expect from them and listen to what they want to get across, and then I prep them for their in-studio experience. I have to juggle it all to produce the best show possible.

Many of the chefs' stories you'll read in this book have emerged from my quest to find and tell interesting stories about America's most talented chefs. It's the deep knowledge and creative energies of these artists that fuels my professional life, and many of my personal pleasures as well. I've built the Rolodex as well as the relationships with these chefs because I genuinely care about them, and our relationships are about much more than work. They are true friendships.

This book reveals what makes these chefs tick and why food drives them. Some of their stories are based on accomplishments. Others tell how food saved their lives. It's my way of sharing the inside story, the secret ingredients of their lives, and their signature dishes (along with some of their great recipes that you really can make at home). Not all are celebrities, but they're all extraordinary cooks with wonderful stories about how food connects people. No matter who you are, you have to eat. Chow!

Charlie Trotter

When I had the opportunity to dine at the chef's table of Charlie Trotter's namesake restaurant in Chicago, I knew who Charlie was in a heartbeat. He was directing all of the action in that kitchen with the deftness of an orchestra conductor. Every person on the staff was constantly catching his eye, checking for cues, playing to his beat. I've been in a lot of restaurant kitchens since then, and Charlie's is probably the tidiest I've ever seen—everything has a place, the spices are lined up, every pot is polished, glass doors reveal each cabinet's immaculate contents. The spotlessness and order he maintains amidst what would be chaos in another chef's kitchen is a sign of Charlie's control over his kitchen. Not an order comes in or a plate goes out that the man doesn't look over. Witnessing the magic that goes on in Charlie's kitchen is like being at a show.

Dining in Charlie's kitchen was where I had my first experience with a tasting menu. I was still looking for a regular menu when the waiter placed a plate in front of me and explained that he was serving Sonoma foie gras with caramelized kumquats and a terrine of wild mushrooms. Wondering what the heck foie gras was, I eyed the dish, smiled, and swallowed what was probably a three hundred-dollar piece of duck liver in one bite. Then came the marinated yellowfin tuna wrapped in Homa Homa oyster with preserved papaya and shellfish oil, the baby skate wing with brown

butter and hundred-year-old Balsamico, the vegetable ragout with Perigord black truffles and red wine infused vegetable juices—each with the wine to go with it—on through to warm cactus pear and banana soup with yogurt sorbet and a blue cheese soufflé with poached pear and vanilla syrup. Trotter's offers nothing a la carte. Each night there are three degustation menus: Grand, Vegetable, and Kitchen, which are part of his signature dining experience and innovative style of service.

I now realize that a great chef like Charlie is never off duty. He looks at a flower and wonders if it's edible or whether the color might work in a presentation. It always comes around to food, his mind is always working, and quality is always paramount. The average diner might question paying ninety-five dollars per person for his vegetable tasting menu, but it could feature heirloom tomatoes grown locally for the restaurant, Hudson Valley Camembert and petite greens, white asparagus, or truffles. Charlie's whole culinary philosophy revolves around organic ingredients from independent and local sources, selected for quality and freshness. The intense flavors are inspiration for his tasting menus, which reflect his sense of drama and sophistication. It's his unique version of modern American cuisine.

Charlie ended that first extraordinary visit to his restaurant by thanking me for coming and presenting me with a personalized menu listing every delicacy he'd prepared that evening. I was very honest, and said, "You know Charlie, I know television, but I don't know food." He said, "Anything you want to know, call me." I told him that he shouldn't have told me that, because I'd take him up on it, and I did.

About four months later the network had really taken off and I was ready to start booking chefs and lining up stories for a show called "Food News and Views." This new assignment basically meant that I had to learn everything I didn't know about the culinary world: about wine and cooking schools and the tools of the trade, plus a thousand other things. When I consulted Charlie for advice, I told him I didn't need to be an expert, but I needed to be able to play the game. He recommended books, told me to subscribe to *Food & Wine* and *Gourmet*, put me in touch with his purveyors, and gave me contacts and story leads. Chefs don't give out information from their coveted rolodexes casually, but he was keen to give me a boost and prepare me for this big culinary adventure I was about to embark on.

Charlie's was one of the first chef profiles I did on the show. Although Charlie didn't attend a culinary institute, he'd always known he wanted to be in food, even well before cooking was considered cool. Charlie was one of the founding fathers of the school of thought that service is as important a part of the dining experience as food, an attitude that used to be strictly European. Charlie holds a regular class to teach his waiters how to respond to diners' needs and attend to detail, with instructions ranging from how to pour wine and remove plates to how to wipe a water glass. The staff inspects every piece of silverware three times before it goes on the table. His restaurant serves only eighty people or so, and it's staffed by educated sommeliers and those who have dedicated their lives to expert service. Diners are treated like royalty, and guests who've eaten at Charlie Trotter's and appreciated what he has to offer join an exclusive fraternity. It's a very polished, highly evolved experience.

When I asked how it had all happened, his answer was simply, "Dedication. You have to be dedicated in going after what you want and what you want to give back." I've never met more of a hands-on chef. Charlie won't hesitate to show the new guy on the kitchen crew the right way to clean lettuce. He's also a perfectionist. If the garnish isn't perfect, he'll get a fresh piece, place it exactly where he envisions it, and you really can see the difference. He expects his level of perfectionism from everyone on his staff.

Charlie brings the same perfectionism to his successful television show, "Kitchen Sessions with Charlie Trotter." He built the television studio kitchen inside his office, which is connected to the restaurant. In the course of a day he'll prep for the show, go over the day's menu with his sous-chef, get his make-up on and tape the show, and return to the restaurant when the bell rings for pre-meal. He moves back and forth between camera-friendly teacher and commander of the kitchen, remaining focused and keeping track of his priorities.

I met Charlie's wife, Lynn, during my trip to Chicago, which was right after their son, Dylan, was born. There's no denying that Charlie is one busy man, but he's never too busy for Lynn and Dylan, who spend a lot of time in the restaurant. Lynn has always helped Charlie, either in the kitchen or the office, and Charlie is very close to his son. At one point Charlie had a trampoline in his back yard, and in the early nineties he'd go out an jump on it to let off steam and extra energy. These days Charlie runs marathons to keep his mind, body, and spirit connected. You might even catch the serious chef doing a perfect handstand at the end of a successful work day, after every patron has left the building. But when he'sin that kitchen, there's no messing around. Everybody is intensely busy, and the talk is all about the food: what's on the tasting menu, how the duck is going to be prepped, even who the guests are that day.

His crew also works very hard, but Charlie makes them feel valued. Every May he comes to New York City for the James Beard Awards—the Academy Awards of the food world—and I take him around to try new places and meet chefs on the rise. Charlie doesn't just bring Lynn, he brings ten or twelve of his staff. If he wins a James Beard Award, he feels it's something he and his team accomplished together, and they know it.

Charlie also gives back in many other ways. He could put his restaurant anywhere in the world, yet instead of renting space in a four-star hotel or a posh commercial district, he's chosen to be part of the fabric of a Chicago neighborhood, in a brownstone in Lincoln Park. He could buy fresh ingredients—goat cheese, herbs, mushrooms—from anywhere in the world, but he goes out of his way to keep smaller farmers and growers, who have a direct connection to the land, in business. In addition, he's a food activist who champions sustainable agriculture.

Introducing children to fine cuisine is another one of Charlie's passions. He offers kids whose only other restaurant experience might be eating at McDonald's or T.G.I.Friday's a chance to taste his food. Two nights a week, the restaurant opens early, so high school students in the Chicago area can tour the kitchen during prep time. Not only does he serve them a full tasting menu, he explains how to order from a regular menu and talks to them about why they should try new things and what the food is all about.

The culinary world is close knit. When Patrick Clark, the great chef of New York City's Tavern on the Green, died of heart disease in 1998, he left behind a wife and five children. I helped put together a fundraising tribute, and Charlie was one of the first chefs to sign up—I didn't even have to call him. At events like this the sponsor of the event supplies the plates and the water, vintners donate the wine, and the chef provides everything else. Charlie was auctioning off dinner and wine for a private party of twelve, and two men were engaged in a bidding war. When the price got up to ten thousand five hundred dollars, Charlie jumped up and said, "Hey, it's for my man Patrick—I'll do it for both of you." He had to come back from Chicago, with staff and food—twice! And if he misses two days a month at his restaurant, that's a lot. Charlie is extremely serious about his work and craft, but beneath that crisp white chef's jacket lies a heart of gold—or perhaps of caviar and foie gras!

Cold Curried-Cucumber Soup

Makes 4 appetizer servings

- 1 tablespoon vegetable oil
- 2 tablespoons minced fresh ginger
- 10 scallions, (use white parts and ⅔ of the green portion), cleaned and chopped
- 5 medium cucumbers, peeled, seeded, and chopped, (about 10 cups)
- ½ cup rice wine vinegar
- 2½ cups chicken stock
- 1½ teaspoons curry powder
- Salt and freshly ground pepper
- 1 cup whole-milk yogurt
- 2 teaspoons chopped fresh basil

Heat the vegetable oil in a medium saucepan, then add the ginger and scallions and sauté over medium heat for about 4 minutes, stirring frequently. Add the cucumbers, vinegar, chicken stock, and curry powder, and stirring occasionally, simmer for 15 minutes. Reserve 1 cup of the cooked cucumber mixture, then puree the remaining cucumber with the cooking liquid in a blender or food processor. Chill the puree for 2 to 3 hours.

Once the soup is chilled, whisk in the yogurt and season to taste with salt and freshly ground pepper.

Place some of the reserved cucumber in the center of each bowl and pour the chilled soup on top. Sprinkle each serving with the basil and top with more freshly ground pepper.

Emeril Lagasse

Emeril Lagasse has been with the Food Network since it was created. In April of 1995 I met him in the network's green room. I knew who he was because I'd heard the network executives talking about the "hot chef from New Orleans." Originally they created a show for him called "How to Boil Water," but the corny format didn't suit Emeril's style. Still, they knew he had potential. Not all chefs are great on television, but when Emeril gets in front of a camera, magic happens. Whether the subject is food or music or sports, viewers want to learn but don't want to sit through a lecture. Emeril makes learning about food fun, and he doesn't hold himself up as the ultimate authority.

Emeril's background is part of modern-day culinary folklore. He grew up in a middle-class family in Fall River, Massachusetts, raised by a Portuguese mother and a French-Canadian father. During high school he worked in a Portuguese bakery and mastered the art of baking bread and pastry. Emeril also taught himself how to play the trombone and flute. However, his real love was the drums, and he was talented enough to receive a full scholarship to the Berklee School of Music in Boston. It was a tremendous opportunity, and it was rough telling Hilda and Mr. John—that's what Emeril calls his parents—that he was turning it down to attend the College of Culinary Arts at Johnson and Wales University in Providence, Rhode Island. He had to work at a banquet-style restaurant to put himself through college, and although his parents were more than a little surprised, they encouraged him to follow his instincts.

After graduating, Emeril worked in several restaurants along the East Coast and in Paris before getting the call, when he was only twenty-six years old, to replace Paul Prudhomme at Commander's Palace, a famous Cajun restaurant in New Orleans. The job entailed learning the ABCs of Creole cooking, and Emeril fell in love with the people and culture of New Orleans. After serving as the executive chef at Commander's Palace for seven and a half years, Emeril opened his own restaurant in March of 1990. Called Emeril's, it was one of the first institutions to give Commander's Palace a run for its money as a New Orleans fine dining experience. He decided to locate in the city's warehouse district, a risky move at the time because there were no other restaurants in the neighborhood. But Emeril wanted more space for his dollar and gambled that the diners would come to him, and they did.

Emeril calls his style of cooking "New" New Orleans Cuisine. He uses traditional Creole recipes but incorporates flavors from Asia, Italy, and other parts of the United States. Beignets, for example, the tasty fried-dough New Orleans-style doughnuts typically dipped in powdered sugar—are stuffed with eggplant and shrimp in Emeril's kitchen. He'll put rabbit in his gumbo or use upscale ingredients like duck and wild mushrooms to create a signature gumbo. You also might find Emeril stuffing Louisiana crayfish with farm-raised quail and serving it with a sweet corn relish and braised red cabbage.

When Emeril was in the studio that day in April to shoot a pilot for "The Essence of Emeril," we started chatting. He was genuinely interested in the duties of a producer, and we talked for over an hour and a half. I had just been assigned a story called "The Inside Scoop on a Chef's Day" and explained that I had to find a chef who would let me spend the day in his restaurant—from 5 A.M. until closing time—whereupon he suggested Emeril's, his flagship restaurant in New Orleans. I had to laugh at the notion that the show would pay my way there with all the chefs available in New York, but Emeril's response was, "If you really want to learn, I'll sponsor your trip."

I accepted Emeril's offer, and arrived in New Orleans two weeks later. He had a driver pick me up at the airport, and his assistant explained that I was to meet him at the restaurant at 11 P.M. to scout the location. It seemed a little late, but I went by and met all the people at the restaurant, who were starting to close down for the night. After work the crew often went out for a drink and invited me along, so at midnight we headed down the street to a hole-in-the-wall bar. We sat outside on plastic chairs, and I drank a beer, then a rum and coke, then another, then another, at which point Emeril looked at his watch and said, "Oh Roche, you better go home and get some rest, because call time tomorrow is 5 A.M." It was one-thirty in the morning, and Emeril had completely set me up.

I got to the shoot, met the cameraman, and got dressed in my borrowed chef's whites. Emeril came in at six o'clock and his energy was off the charts—he was completely different from the relaxed guy I'd shared drinks with the night before. The first item of the day was to review the previous night's business; then Emeril had to check the refrigerator, figure out what was coming in fresh that morning, and draw up the day's tasting menu and specials. I watched Emeril and the sous-chef while they discussed their plans for that night's menu. In less than twenty minutes they factored taste, texture, prep time, and availability into deciding how these raw ingredients would be turned into special dishes by evening.

One item on that menu was a field green salad with organic heirloom tomatoes and herbs with a sprinkle of extra virgin olive oil. My job as a prep cook was to slice the tomatoes for the salad. But the restaurant has as many as two hundred covers a night, and I had to prep for one hundred and fifty of those salads. It was one of the most tedious things I had ever done. The tomatoes had to be sliced and quartered in a certain way, and when I'd get a little sloppy, Emeril would know it from across the room and come back and demonstrate the proper technique again. I kept thinking, "And this is just the tomatoes." I started around 7:30 A.M. and didn't finish until 1:30 P.M. (It probably would have taken a more experienced person an hour and a half.) My next job turned out to be to tag along with the saucier, who was stirring, sautéing, and reducing the sauces of the day over the large Vulcan stove, which had burners the size of home plate. The heat by the stove was unbearable, and after a few minutes I looked like I had just stepped out of the shower. We'd gotten all the sauces started by 2:30 P.M. or so, when it was time to have lunch.

Different people alternate cooking lunch for the crew and what is served is not necessarily what they serve in the restaurant. Instead, meals that go a long way, like macaroni and cheese and baked chicken, are made. It's like a family meal at which the forty-five or so staffers eat together, and at that point I was so grateful to be able to sit down, if only for thirty minutes. Then, filled with newfound respect for everyone who spends all day in that hot

kitchen, I got to sit in Emeril's office. I listened to him conduct his business: talking to purveyors, interviewing a new employee, fine-tuning the menu. Around 4 P.M. Emeril conducted what he calls "pre-meal." Everyone came into the dining room, we all started clapping, Emeril thanked us all for being there and ran through the evening's events: who's coming, what they eat, their likes and dislikes. "Michael Jordan will be in the Wine Room, doing a special tasting menu. We want champagne waiting at the table. . ." and so on. It was like a play rehearsal, with Emeril running through each person's part in making that experience right for each guest. Energy and ideas flowed as we prepared for the doors to open at six o'clock. The meeting ended with everyone clapping and cheering, newly focused and energized to face a busy night.

Back in the kitchen my job was to put the tomatoes on the salad. I wouldn't say it was hard, but the slices had to go in a particular place. After Emeril sent back the third salad, I got it right. I worked that salad station until 11 P.M. When I left, Emeril stood at the door and said, "I'll see you tomorrow but as my guest."

I knew that at the next day's pre-meal they'd say, "Rochelle Brown is coming!" Sure enough, the staff greeted me warmly and escorted me and my friends Dana and Kate to the chef's bar. Since there's a two-month waiting list to get a seat at that bar, the other diners were wondering who we were. The dinner reservation was for 6:30 P.M., and we did not leave until 2 A.M. The quail stuffed with cornbread and andouille dressing was one of the best dishes I'd ever had, and the barbecued shrimp appetizer with rosemary biscuits is a dish I crave to this day. We also had pan-seared escolar (a fish in the mackerel family that Emeril popularized) with crabmeat and chanterelles, and seared duck with caramelized onion bread. The onion bread had the consistency of sweet bread pudding, but it's savory and dissolves right in your mouth.

For dessert Emeril sent out a platter with twelve different desserts, enough to feed half the restaurant. It included praline cream pie, Grand Marnier chocolate soufflé, pecan pie, vanilla praline ice cream, plus watermelon, lemon, and coconut sorbets, to lighten things up a bit. That was also my introduction to Emeril's decadent banana cream pie with chocolate shavings and caramel sauce, which I regularly ask him to make for me. He layers fresh bananas and cream filling, covers it with chocolate shavings and whipped cream, and tops it off with caramel sauce. As Emeril says, "It makes your taste buds happy, happy, happy." Just as we figured the meal was finally over, Emeril, the sous-chef, and the house manager served us what they call a "nightcap." "Hello ladies! To finish off the night," Emeril declared with a flourish, "here we have my chocolate Martini with chocolate grapes"—small white grapes covered with semi-sweet chocolate, served in a Martini glass over shaved ice and vodka, with a splash of Chambord. The dinner was out of this world and so was the service. If I made a move, a waiter would be there to pull out my chair. As I reached for my water glass, someone would wipe the sweat from my glass. And did I mention that we had a different wine with every course? We practically needed a wheelbarrow to carry us home.

Over the next few years Emeril and I stayed in touch socially, but it was not until 1997 that we reconnected. The show I was producing at the time was cancelled and Emeril's show was being revamped and he needed a new producer. When Emeril asked me to produce "Emeril Live!" I knew I was being given an extraordinary opportunity. Keeping up with Emeril, however, is no mean feat. It's not unusual for him to wake up at 2 A.M. to do a live "Good Morning America" segment and then come over to the Food Network studios to tape three live one-hour shows that feature more than eighteen recipes. After that he'll take his wife, Alden, to dinner and check in with the staff at each of his restaurants before calling it a day. Yet he finds time for telephone interviews between segments, visiting with special-needs children at the end of every show, and being an exceptional friend.

Despite having two successful shows on the Food Network, six popular cookbooks, seven restaurants, and a line of cookware and spices, Emeril is a remarkably warm, down-to-earth person, even humble. He's able to run all of these operations out of his New Orleans office because he goes out of his way to make each person he works with—whether receptionist, agent, business manager, or producer—feel like an important and respected member of the team.

Emeril continues to open my eyes to new ways to cook, serve, and season while continuously challenging me to bring fresh, inter-

esting culinary ideas into the studio. And when I don't know something, he never makes me feel like it's anything but his pleasure to educate me yet again. Emeril has captured the heart of Americans in a way that nobody since Julia Child has done. People say, "I can't believe my cleaning lady and my boss both love this guy," and I say, "Emeril can be anyone's neighbor." Whether he's in front of the camera or behind the stove, with Emeril what you see is what you get. And America loves that.

Alden's Kicked-Up Cornbread

Makes 12 servings

½ pound bacon, diced
1¼ cups all-purpose flour
¾ cup enriched cornmeal
2 teaspoons baking powder
1 teaspoon salt
1 cup grated Cheddar cheese
1½ cups buttermilk
¼ cup vegetable oil
2 whole eggs, beaten

Preheat the oven to 400°F.

Place the chopped bacon in a 10-inch cast-iron skillet over medium heat. Render the bacon, stirring often, until most of the fat has released and the meat is crisp, 7 to 8 minutes. Remove the bacon from the skillet, and set aside, then transfer the pan with the bacon fat to the oven.

Combine the flour, cornmeal, baking powder, and salt with the Cheddar cheese, then stir in the buttermilk, vegetable oil, and eggs, mixing until dry ingredients are just moistened. Fold the bacon into this batter.

Remove the skillet from the oven, and pour the batter into the pan. Bake for 25 to 30 minutes, or until the cornbread is a light golden brown and a wooden toothpick inserted into its center comes out clean. Cut into wedges and serve warm.

Lidia Bastianich

Next to a long line of people waiting to speak to Julia Child at the housewares convention in Chicago was a short, animated woman doing a great demonstration of Cuisinart's newest line of stainless steel cookware. Although her audience wasn't as big as Julia's, people were paying close attention because it was clear from her warm and authoritative manner that she cared about what she was doing. Lidia was preparing little handmade ravioli stuffed with sage, and people were captivated by her manner and by what she was allowing them to taste. After everybody had eaten and left, I went up to her and introduced myself.

She told me she had a restaurant in New York City, and I told her about my job with the Food Network. I interviewed Lidia about my assignment—food trends, and her thoughts on the new network. Unlike a lot of the merchandisers at the show who were only interested in what I could do for them, Lidia was interested in my questions and how she could help this new enterprise. There's a lot of arrogance in the food world, and I was lucky that

the first person I met was generous with her expertise. Although my ignorance was painfully apparent, Lidia wasn't condescending—she treated me as a fellow professional, albeit one with a lot of learning to do. By the time we parted, I had the feeling that I had made a valuable contact and begun a real friendship.

About a year later I had the opportunity to interview her for a series on the Food Network about the new Italian-American cuisine. Most chefs talk about where they went to school, but Lidia wasn't classically trained. She learned how to cook from her grandmother, as a child growing up in Pola, a town on the southwestern tip of Istria, a peninsula about ninety miles northeast of Venice. She came to the United States to go to college, wound up marrying, and she and her husband opened up two small Italian restaurants in Queens. Lidia made it her business to become the sous-chef. She wanted to keep it classic Italian cuisine, because Lidia's mission is all about preserving her heritage. To this day, her objective is to give every diner a consistently authentic meal because of her infectious passion about representing her culture through food. She's not using a measuring cup; she knows it takes a little of this, a pinch of that to bring her grandmother's teachings to the stove and to the table.

When you step into her restaurant, Felidia, located on 58th Street in New York City, the smells of sauces simmering and breads baking hit you immediately. Lidia walks through the dining room and warmly greets guests, making you feel like you're with family. Her son Joe runs Becco and Esca, her other restaurants in

Manhattan, and he projects the same kindness in the dining room as his mother.

We spent a whole week at Felidia shooting for the television series, and we saw many different sides of Lidia—mother, chef, restaurateur, cookbook author, mentor. At the time I was feeling a great deal of stress. As a start-up we didn't have a big staff, and I was producing six to eight stories a week. These chefs have grueling schedules and their hours had become mine as well, and I wasn't sure I could keep it up. The bonus on these shoots was that you got to eat. One lunchtime Lidia and I sat together, and she asked gently, "Are you okay?" I opened up and confessed, "I'm not doing half as much as you, but I'm feeling worn out, and I'm not sure I'm doing justice to my subjects." She said, "I'm going to order for you," and while we sat there she confirmed that I loved what I did, assured me I had talent, and told me to snap out of it. She said, "You have to create a mission for yourself, not for the network or the chefs, and if at the end of the day you've done the best you could, no one can ask for more." I realized that my own expectations had become unreasonable, and that was a turning point. And when she saw me putting away her delicious, comforting lasagna she smiled—she'd pulled it off again.

Lidia is one of the few great chefs who is also a brilliant entrepreneur. She oversees three major restaurants in New York City, each dedicated to her principles of simplicity and the best ingredients. She makes the decisions in all three restaurant kitchens and doesn't just put her name on things other people have done. She leads culinary tours to Italy that are driven by the same desire to show people where her food originates. She takes them to where the olive oils are made and the recipes come from, to fancy restaurants and mom-and-pop trattorias. She has two popular shows on PBS, "Lidia's Italian Table" and "Lidia's Italian-American Kitchen" where she teaches great dishes that you can actually make at home. Because of the nature of my job, I get a lot of invitations to charity benefits, and nine times out of ten one of Lidia's restaurants is involved. She uses all of these vehicles to get her message out to as many people as she can.

Lidia was the first female chef I did a series on, and she and her ambitious enterprises are still remarkable. Not to mention pulling this off in New York City, where so many three- and four-star chefs compete for patrons on a daily basis. She knows what she's good at and enjoys sharing what she knows. Lidia is also the only woman I've ever worked with on television who is never worried about her appearance. Her focus is always on the food.

■■ ■ ■■ ■

Chicken Bites with Potatoes, Sausages, and Vinegar
Bocconcini di Pollo con Patate e Salsicce

Makes 6 servings

2 frying chickens (about 3 pounds each, preferably free range)
¼ cup extra virgin olive oil
½ pound sweet Italian sausage
   Salt and freshly ground pepper
1 cup onions, roughly cut into 1-inch pieces
1 cup red or yellow peppers, cut into 1-inch pieces
1 pound small red bliss potatoes (about 12), washed and
   cut in half
6 garlic cloves, peeled
3 sprigs fresh rosemary
¼ cup red wine vinegar
2 tablespoons chopped fresh Italian parsley, leaves only for garnish

Cut each chicken into twelve pieces. Wash and pat the chicken pieces dry, then season them generously with salt and pepper. Preheat the oven to 450°F.

Heat 2 tablespoons of the olive oil in a wide, heavy skillet over medium heat. Add the sausage and cook, turning often until lightly browned on all sides, about 3 minutes for thinner sausages or 5 minutes for wider sausages. Remove the sausage pieces with a slotted spoon and transfer them to a roasting pan or baking dish large enough to hold all the sausage, chicken and potatoes and allow room for stirring. (An 18- by 15-inch roasting pan is ideal.) Generously season the chicken with salt and pepper. Increase the heat to medium-high and add as many chicken pieces, skin side down, as will fit in a single layer. Cook, turning once, until well browned on both sides, about 8 minutes, then transfer to the roasting pan. Add the remaining chicken pieces as room becomes available. When all the chicken has been browned, add the onions and pepper, mix well. Add the potatoes, cut side down and cook until browned, about 6–8 minutes. Transfer the remaining chicken pieces, onions, peppers, and potatoes.

Whack the garlic cloves with the flat side of a knife to crush them and scatter the garlic and the rosemary over the contents of the roasting pan. Drizzle with the remaining 2 tablespoons oil and roast 15 minutes, stirring gently occasionally. Sprinkle the chicken, sausage, and potato mixture with the vinegar and continue roasting, stirring gently occasionally, until all ingredients are browned, the chicken is cooked through, and the potatoes are very tender, about 15 minutes.

Prop up one end of the roasting pan and let rest 5 minutes. Spoon off the excess fat, sprinkle with the parsley, and transfer to a warm serving platter. Serve immediately.

■ ■ ■

Daniel Boulud

In 1993 Daniel Boulud left New York City's famed celebrity haunt Le Cirque to open his own restaurant, called Daniel.

The only thing I'd heard about him up until then was that he was a truly great French chef who had trained under legendary French masters Roger Vergé, Georges Blanc, and Michel Guérard. There was a lot of buzz when his new restaurant opened, but it wasn't until 1997 that Emeril Lagasse took me there as part of my culinary education. Just stepping into the dining room was an experience. The decor was extremely elegant, linen dazzlingly white and crisp, waiters in green blazers. At that point I hadn't been to Europe, but that night I felt as though I had stepped out of the streets of New York and into Paris.

The waiter pulled out my chair, we sat down, I picked up the menu, and Emeril said, "What are you looking at that for? We're going to have Daniel cook for us." That meant we'd be served what is in essence a customized tasting menu, a variety of dishes personally prepared by the chef. Because I was with Emeril, it also meant a sinful amount of food—eight courses in all. When a chef offers a tasting menu, he is presenting his best dishes. He pours his heart into this menu, so you graciously accept whatever is put in front of you—you don't say, "No thank you."

The first dish was an asparagus soup—a dish I have never liked. However, I cleaned the bowl; it was delicious. It was as though Daniel was opening my horizons from the very beginning. The second course consisted of huge, caramelized scallops topped with beluga caviar. Knowing I wasn't a big caviar fan, Emeril shot me this look that said, "You *will* like it." I'd just done a story on

caviar and I figured I could pop the beluga into a Ziploc bag and pay my rent with it, but I knew I had to eat it. I grew up eating fried seafood, so I clearly recall the intense salty burst of the caviar and the way it then harmonized with the delicate flesh of the pan-seared scallop.

As the courses kept coming, accompanied by French wines picked by Emeril, the anticipation only heightened. I went from wondering, "Is this going to be something for me?" to "This *is* me." One of my favorite dishes in the world is one Daniel served us that night called Sea Scallops in Black Tie: Maine sea scallops layered with black truffles in a golden pastry. (I learned that it's not uncommon to have the same ingredient prepared several different ways during the course of the meal. The chef wants you to taste the best of the best. He's showing off his versatility.) The presentation was spectacular too. At Daniel, you can almost see the flavor before you taste it. At the end of the meal, Daniel came out to our table, his apron spotless even though he'd been in the kitchen all night. He shook my hand and said, "I hope you had enough to eat." All I could say was, "Thank you, thank you, thank you." Although his palate is enormously sophisticated, Daniel made French cuisine and French chefs approachable to me that night.

That dinner was one of my most memorable food experiences. It had a lot to do with Emeril's guidance. As a chef, Emeril could explain why a certain cheese was exceptional, or that the foie gras and apple appetizer worked so well because the acidity of the apple balanced the richness of the foie gras. He explained that Daniel sets a standard for excellence in classic French cuisine, as a master of traditional techniques. The twist is often in the choice of ingredients, which celebrates nature's seasonal bounty.

Daniel was born on a farm outside Lyons, the gastronomic capital of France. He was raised on home-cooked meals prepared on the basis of what was growing in the family garden at the time, or what game was in season. In the same way, Daniel frequently reworks the restaurant's menu from top to bottom as different ingredients come into season. For catered events the menu is often decided upon only a week in advance; the dishes are dictated by the availability of ingredients, which are purchased the day before the event. Daniel's ability to craft well-rounded tempting menus out of unanticipated ingredients is a hallmark of his culinary genius.

My first opportunity to work with him on television came in 2000, when we did a show on patés and terrines. I had been warned that Daniel might be difficult to work with, because he's very serious about his food and his craft, but he was totally the opposite. His restaurant rates four stars in the *New York Times* and is considered one of the best in the world. He also runs the more casual Café Boulud and DB Bistro Moderne, operates the catering business, Feast and Fêtes, and writes cookbooks, so he's incredibly busy. But Daniel doesn't have the oversized ego to match these accomplishments.

For the television program he made a terrine with layers of mushrooms, spinach, and duck; an oxtail-artichoke-foie gras terrine with black truffles; a terrine of squab and foie gras with onion compote topped with sliced toasted almonds and puree of sweet roasted tomato; and a terrine of duck foie gras with a cranberry-apple sauce, using a whole variety of techniques. And he rolled out the good stuff. There are no substitutions for quality when Daniel cooks. He has a whole philosophy of full-bodied food from the region he grew up in, which he combines with ingredients from his adopted country. And while his classical approach to preparing these foods has really put him where he is today, he combines layers and tastes into dishes that are highly original.

The typical restaurant kitchen is all utilitarian stainless steel and bright lights, but at Daniel it's more like a kitchen in a French home only on a grand scale—big copper pots hanging from ceiling racks, colorful sea green and sunny yellow tiles on the walls, warm lighting—as though he wants to be in a beautiful space to make beautiful things. His grandmother taught him how to start a garden and grow his own food. His eyes sparkled as he said, "Some boys are excited to play with their new Matchbox car, but it was cooking with my grandmother that brought me that excitement." At the turn of the century, Daniel's great-grandparents began providing a venue on their property outside Lyons for people to come together to celebrate major events in the life of the community, and it came to be known as Café Boulud.

Daniel brought Café Boulud to New York City in 1998 because he wanted people here to taste the treasured recipes he'd grown up on, the food that made him who he is as a person as well as a cook. The menu pays tribute to the chef's four culinary muses: "*La Tradition*, the classic dishes of French cooking; *La Saison*, the seasonal specialties of the market; *Le Potager*, a celebration of the vegetable garden; and *Le Voyage*, the exotic flavors of world cuisines." Daniel has entrusted the kitchen of Café Boulud to Andrew Carmellini, himself an award-winning chef.

After the September eleventh attack on the World Trade Center, I was working on a Food Network special to rally support for New York City restaurants. Daniel was one of the chefs I selected to interview for the special, and we talked about why he had chosen to live and cook in this city out of all the great cities in the world. Daniel cited New Yorkers' support of fine dining, the open-mindedness of the diners, the city's renowned culinary reputation, and the incredible array of ingredients available. But after more than eighteen years in the Big Apple, Daniel has done more than pour his talents into dining establishments that reflect his country of origin—he's made New York City his home.

Saffron-Flavored Mussel Velouté with Gratin of Mussels

Makes 4 servings

For the mussels

 1 tablespoon unsalted butter
 3 shallots, thinly sliced, rinsed, and dried
 2 pounds mussels, scrubbed
1½ cups dry white wine
 Freshly ground pepper

Melt 1 tablespoon of the butter in a Dutch oven or large casserole over medium heat. Add the shallots and cook, stirring, until they just turn translucent, about 5 minutes. Add the mussels and turn the heat to high. Pour in the white wine, season with a little pepper, and put the lid on the pot. While the mussels are cooking, give the pot a few shakes or stir the mussels a couple of times with a slotted spoon to help them cook evenly. Cook until the mussel shells just open, 3 to 4 minutes. When all the mussel shells have popped, turn them into a large, cheesecloth-lined sieve set over a bowl to catch the flavorful cooking liquid. Reserve the broth (you should have about 8 cups).

As soon as the mussels are cool enough to handle, remove the meat from the shells and pull off and discard any black fibers attached to the mussels; discard the shells and any shallots in the sieve too. Set the mussels aside, covered, or you can refrigerate them overnight if you plan to serve the dish the next day.

For the velouté

2 tablespoons unsalted butter
2 tablespoons extra virgin olive oil
2 onions, thinly sliced
1 fennel bulb, trimmed and thinly sliced
2 stalks celery, peeled, trimmed, and thinly sliced
1 leek, white and light green parts only, thinly sliced, washed, and dried
1 large carrot, peeled, trimmed, and thinly sliced
3 large, ripe beefsteak tomatoes, peeled, seeded, and chopped
 Large pinch of saffron
 Sachet (1 teaspoon fennel seeds, 1 teaspoon coriander seeds, 1 teaspoon white peppercorns, 1 bay leaf, 2 sprigs fresh thyme, and 4 sprigs fresh Italian parsley all tied in cheesecloth)
1 cup heavy cream
8 cups mussel broth (reserved above)
4 cups unsalted chicken stock or store-bought, low-sodium chicken broth
 Salt and freshly ground pepper

Melt the butter and olive oil in a large pot. Add the onions and cook, stirring until they just turn translucent, 5 to 7 minutes. Add the fennel, celery, leek, carrot, and tomatoes, and cook until the vegetables are tender, about 15 minutes. Add the saffron, sachet, heavy cream, mussel broth, and chicken stock. Taste and season with salt and pepper. Bring the mixture to a boil and cook for 20 minutes more. Be assiduous about skimming.

Transfer the soup to the container of a blender. (Depending on the size of your blender, you may have to work in batches.) Puree the soup, then push it through a fine-mesh sieve to create the velouté. Add more salt and pepper if needed. The velouté can be cooled, transferred to an airtight container, and refrigerated for 4 days or frozen for a month. Bring to a boil again before serving.

For the parsley-garlic crust

¾ cup fresh breadcrumbs
½ cup plus 2 tablespoons unsalted butter, softened
2 tablespoons finely chopped Italian parsley, leaves only
4 cloves garlic, germ removed and finely chopped
1 tablespoon finely chopped toasted almonds
 Salt and freshly ground pepper

Mix together the breadcrumbs, butter, parsley, garlic, and almonds; season with salt and pepper. Roll out the breadcrumb-butter mixture between two pieces of parchment paper to form a square approximately 4 by 4 inches and ⅛ to ¼ inch thick. Place the packet in the freezer for at least a half hour. Remove and cut into four small squares; refrigerate until needed.

To make the gratins: Preheat the broiler. Butter four shallow gratin dishes, about 1-inch deep and 6 inches in diameter. Divide the reserved mussels among the gratin dishes using a 2-inch ring to place them neatly in the center of each dish. Remove the ring, peel the breadcrumb-butter squares off the parchment paper, and place one on top of each gratin. Bake underneath the broiler for 2 to 4 minutes—watch them closely to avoid burning them—or until the tops are golden brown.

Using a spatula, place the hot mussel gratins in the center of four warm bowls. Ladle the hot soup around the mussels and serve immediately.

Marcus Samuelsson

As part of the Food Network's Black History Month series in 1995, I had pitched a round table on what it is to be a black chef in America, and I had to come up with some great African-American chefs for my panel. I was looking through the usual newspapers and magazines, and there in the lifestyle section of *USA Today* was a mention of a Marcus Samuelsson. I was surprised to find out that he was a fellow GenXer right here in New York City, yet I'd never heard of him. I put down my tea and bagel, called Aquavit, a three-star Scandinavian restaurant in midtown, introduced myself, and asked to speak to the chef. You can never expect to get the chef on the phone, but Marcus is always thinking ahead. When he heard the words "Food Network," he figured it might be an opportunity for him and picked up.

Marcus and I hit it off right away. We were both of African descent, twenty-five years old and in the food game—three unlikely matches. He loved my passion for television and I loved his ability to teach me more about food, so it was a give-and-take relationship from the start. Because we were both so young, we never had to pretend to know something we didn't—we were on the same playing field. The word "gravlax" sounded so strange to me, but I remember Marcus's smile as he explained the various Swedish pickling processes. He and I spent a lot of time together, talking, shopping, eating. We could be at Sylvia's in Harlem on Tuesday, at an Ethiopian restaurant called Meskerem in the West 40s on Wednesday, and the next day at McDonald's for a Big Mac.

Marcus was born in Ethiopia. His parents died of a tuberculosis plague when he was three. A Swedish nurse fell in love with him and his sister in a Swedish field hospital and found a young couple in Göteborg, Sweden, to adopt them. The grandmother was a professional cook, and Marcus was six years old when she started teaching him classical Swedish dishes like meatballs, gravlax, and herring. In Sweden you have to pick a career right after high school, and Marcus chose culinary school. After he completed school in Sweden, he apprenticed in Switzerland, Austria, and France—chefs travel to see how people use different ingredients, or the same ingredients in different ways, to create a superior world cuisine. And, as Marcus discovered, it's also a great way to get hands-on training with the best in the world.

At one point he worked on a cruise ship, and met someone in the food world who told him that the owner of a restaurant in New York City called Aquavit was looking for a sous-chef to raise the profile of fine Scandinavian food in America. So in 1994 Marcus came to New York, met Aquavit's owner, Håkan Swahn, and executive chef, Jan Sendel, and accepted an eight-month internship at the restaurant. Jan and young Marcus were going to create a dream team and revamp the menu when, just eight weeks into this creative partnership, Jan died of a heart attack. This was personally devastating for Marcus, and overnight he had to rise to the challenge of becoming sous-chef. He did so admirably, and in May of 1995, he was appointed executive chef. Three months later, he won a coveted three stars from the *New York Times*, and that's when the article ran that brought him to my attention. I'd never seen a chef get as much buzz as Marcus did in such a short time. Although the media seemed struck by his African heritage, Marcus saw himself as a talented chef who just happened to be Ethiopian introducing people to great Swedish cuisine.

Marcus gave me the chance to see a chef in action outside of the restaurant. One day he took me on a cook's tour of Chinatown, shopping that night's menu. We jumped on the N train to Canal Street, and the first thing I noticed was that all the proprietors of these little food stalls knew him! Although Marcus speaks five languages, Chinese isn't one of them, yet he could clearly communicate with these shopkeepers in the language of food. They were happy to show him the best-quality produce saved in the back room for favored customers. We took a cab back to Midtown with cod still flopping in the bag, basil, thyme, coriander, bok choy, vegetables I hadn't even heard of, and he knew exactly how he was going to combine all these flavors and textures and colors. He was assembling the ingredients with which to create the evening's works of art.

Marcus is a food artist. He regularly visits museums around the city, from the Museum of Modern Art to the Museum for African Art, and he always aspires to be modern in his approach. Different things inspire him—abstract forms, artists' interpretations of landscape, how colors jumping out from a white canvas might be recreated on a white plate. A sculpture in an unconventional pose might inspire him to present the gravlax in a vertical roll on the plate. At Aquavit, each dish is served in a particular style. Foie gras might arrive on a glass block, carrot juice in a test tube. Marcus has even designed his own line of dishes in order to contrast complex creations with his minimalist Scandinavian aesthetic. He uses a painter's brush in the kitchen, putting a slash of tomato-dill aioli on a stark white tureen of mussel soup, or an unexpected dollop of black mustard atop a slice of gravlax. You want to turn the plate, study the contrasts, and memorize the dish before you eat it.

To say Marcus isn't afraid to try new things would be an understatement. Everything about his cuisine is bold, experimental, and artistic. If he does a rhubarb dessert, it's not going to be strawberry-rhubarb pie. It'll be a combination of rhubarb compote, rhubarb sorbet, warm rhubarb jelly over creamy panna cotta, and rhubarb

iced tea, and the dish might look like a painter's palette. Marcus will serve you gravlax with caviar in a vodka shot-glass and the layers make it almost too beautiful to eat. Instead of offering codfish on mashed potatoes, he'll place the fish in a beautiful shallow earthenware bowl on top of whatever greens he found fresh that day. He's assumes total artistic control, from purchasing the ingredients to preparing the dish, plating it, and making sure that each work of art arrives at the table with his intended vision. He's opened a second Aquavit in Minneapolis, a city with a strong Swedish heritage, and recently opened a cafe in New York City's Scandinavian House. Marcus is single-handedly creating a legacy for Swedish cuisine.

In 1999 the press release for the annual James Beard Awards churned out of the fax machine and sure enough, Marcus was nominated for Rising Chef of the Year. When I called him with the news there was a long pause, then, "Are you serious?", which was followed by, "I don't have to win. The nomination just makes me feel so good." We were so happy. Marcus bought his first tuxedo, and that night I picked him up at Aquavit—he worked till the last minute—for a champagne toast at Håkan's house. It was my first time attending the awards as a guest, enjoying the hype I'd helped create, and we watched as a lot of our friends won awards. His category was near the end of the ceremonies. When they announced Marcus's name as the winner I saw a tear escape; he was so touched by all the people who believed in him. And the first person that he thanked was his grandmother back in Sweden.

Tandoori-Smoked Salmon with Citrus Salsa

Makes 4 appetizer servings

For the salmon
1 cup sugar
1/2 cup salt
2 cups water
two 8-ounce salmon fillets with the skin on or off, cleaned and
  trimmed
1 cup wood chips, preferably apple wood
Vegetable oil for the grill
2 tablespoons tandoori spice mix

For the salsa
1 clove garlic, minced
2 tablespoons grapeseed oil
1 teaspoon mustard
2 teaspoons sherry vinegar
1 lime, pink grapefruit, and orange, peeled, seeded, and separated
  into segments
4 fresh mint leaves, finely chopped
4 sprigs fresh cilantro, finely chopped

In a container large enough to immerse the salmon fillets, mix the
sugar and salt in the water until they dissolve. Add the salmon to the
brine and refrigerate for up to 2½ hours. At the same time, in a separate container, cover the wood chips with water and soak them.

When it's almost serving time, remove the salmon from the curing
liquid and pat dry. Drain the wood chips and spread them on the bottom of a stove-top smoker (see Note). Place the tray on top of the
wood chips to catch the juices. Lightly brush the grill with the oil.
Place the fillets, skin side down if you've left the skin on, on top of the
grill. Slide the cover on the smoker and place the whole apparatus on
the stovetop over low heat. Smoke the salmon for 3 minutes.

Turn off the heat, allow the smoker to cool and the smoke to dis-
sipate, then remove the fillets. Rub both sides of the fillets with the
tandoori spice mix to coat, transfer to a platter, and keep warm in a
low-temperature oven.

To prepare the salsa, sauté the garlic in the grapeseed oil over
medium heat, 1 to 2 minutes. Let cool, then add all the remaining
ingredients and toss to combine.

To serve, cut each warm salmon fillet in half and divide among
four serving plates. Top with the citrus salsa.

Note: A stove-top smoker is a rectangular stainless-steel pan
(where you place the wood chips) that includes a tray, a grill, and a
cover. You can find inexpensive versions on the market. You can also
improvise using a wok, a round cake rack of the same dimensions,
and a lid. Line the wok with aluminum foil, shiny side in, before
adding the wood chips.

Rick Bayless

I hate to admit it, but, like most Americans, until I met Rick Bayless I thought of Mexican food as Tex-Mex: guacamole, fajitas, chimichangas, Taco Bell. Rick is the self-appointed savior of Mexican cuisine, banishing that association with fast food and teaching people that chiles flavor a dish in addition to heating it up. Of course most chefs are loyal to their cuisines, but Rick's relationship to his specialty stands out. He knows Mexico inside out—the history of each region and the culture and food that represents it—and when he describes them, you see the gears turning in his mind and his face coming to life. He's an impassioned crusader.

You might not expect such fervor about Mexican cuisine from a guy who grew up in Oklahoma City in a family of restaurateurs who specialized in local barbecue. But Rick studied Spanish and Latin American culture in college and went on to get a doctorate in linguistics from the University of Michigan. While he was at Michigan, a new television show placed an advertisement for a host who was knowledgeable about Mexican food. Egged on by friends who knew him to be a walking encyclopedia on the subject, Rick applied and landed the job, hosting a twenty-six-part PBS television series called "Cooking Mexican" from 1978 to 1979. It was a low-budget operation, so Rick had to do everything from researching and writing to shopping and cooking, but it was a terrific vehicle for getting the word out about the real flavors of Mexico.

At that point Rick was hooked—he knew that he wanted to cook authentic Mexican food. Chefs typically train with experts and follow a pre-existing program, but Rick made his up from scratch. He dedicated five years to traveling across Mexico with his wife, Deann, whom he'd met in graduate school and who can make a mean mole too. Rick's the communicator while Deann is his partner behind the scenes and at the stove. Their daughter Lanie has pretty much grown up in their restaurant. They built a little room for her off the kitchen, so that putting in the long hours didn't mean being apart.

During his Mexican travels, Rick visited farmer's markets, found knowledgeable people to introduce him to local cooks, ate in little places on the side of the road, and took copious notes and many photographs. He needed to do it the hard way, to acquire knowledge and experience on his own so that he could take ownership of what he was going to create. Rick took his first big steps in 1987 when he published his now-classic cookbook, *Authentic Mexican: Regional Cooking from the Heart of Mexico*, and opened up Frontera Grill in Chicago. Frontera Grill specializes in contemporary regional Mexican cooking. It isn't fancy, but it's a long way from Taco Bell. In the beginning people doubted the concept. They'd ask, "What do you mean by fine Mexican cuisine?" Rick let the bold flavors of Mexican food speak for him, and it didn't take long for food writers and critics to start describing the story of his travels and praising the restaurant.

Frontera Grill's adobe-colored walls are covered with masks, paintings, and sculptures Rick picked up during his travels. These artifacts are there as part of Rick's ongoing effort to educate people about the cultural context of the food he makes. It's a small restaurant with around thirty tables, and next door is its sister restaurant, Topolobampo, which offers fine dining in a more elegant setting. Frontera Grill has an open kitchen where you can watch Mexican women making tortillas fresh to order that arrive at your table warm. Rick is obsessive about authenticity. If a recipe calls for a certain type of cactus that he ate in the town where the dish originated, that's what he serves in his restaurant. Substitutions are not acceptable.

It's best to come in with an open mind. A little guidance is helpful, and everyone on the staff is familiar with the history of each dish. Rick came over as I was looking over the smoky peanut mole with grilled quail and Oaxacan black mole with braised chicken. When I pronounced it "mole," he shot me this look through the bottom of his glasses and his teacher instincts kicked right in, the way I bet they do with other diners all evening long. "Rochelle, it's pronounced 'mole-ay,'" he told me, explaining that mole is a complex sauce prepared in many stages, which contains chiles, spices, chocolate, and sometimes other ingredients like sesame and cinnamon. The dark brown sauce sits perfectly on the chicken, in contrast to the whiteness of the plate, and not a drop is out of place.

Rick combines ingredients in a particularly interesting way. He makes tiny tostadas of smoky chicken tinga—a rich tomato-based sauce seasoned with chiles—with avocado and aged cheese. For his Carne Asada, he marinates organic Montana ribeye in spicy red chile sauce, grills it over a wood flame, and serves it with black beans and fried plantains. Then there are his Sopes Surtidos, corn tortilla boats made of masa with a sampler of fillings: chicken in red mole, sweet plantains in sour cream, black beans with homemade chorizo, and guacamole. Rick has invigorated the classic version of guacamole, introducing raw serrano peppers, and variations that use roasted poblanos, tomatoes, and garlic.

These combinations are exciting and unusual to most of us who haven't been exposed to authentic Mexican cuisine served in this fashion. When the meal is over, you've experienced an incredible intensity of flavor, color, and presentation. His Chiles Rellenos—soufflé-battered stuffed poblano peppers, one filled with cheese and one with minced-pork picadillo—have a little burn that perfectly sets off the contrasting flavors of the other ingredients. One of Rick's favorite dishes is Enchiladas de Mole Rojo: homemade tortillas rolled around chicken that's doused with Oaxacan red mole, which is such a deep fire-engine red that it really makes a visual statement in addition to the gastronomic one.

Rick has purveyors grow items specially for him, and he imports many products from Mexico, chiles in particular: smoky chipotle chiles (known for their intense heat); ancho chiles (which are on the sweet side); and arbol chiles (bright orange and very hot). His cookbooks explain where to get these ingredients and what substitutions are acceptable if necessary, which makes the cuisine approachable. Americans used to be afraid to attempt more than beans and rice at home, but Rick demystifies fine Mexican cooking. You don't just get the recipes, you get their history, and it's a history that's not readily available outside Mexico.

Rick set out to prove that Mexican is as viable and important as any other world cuisine, and he has succeeded. He won the

James Beard Award in 1991 for Best American Chef in the Midwest; and in 1995 he won both the Beard Foundation's National Chef of the Year award and the International Association of Culinary Professional's Chef of the Year Award. He has a show on PBS called "Mexico: One Plate at a Time with Rick Bayless"; he's a visiting staff member of the Culinary Institute of America; and he takes groups on culinary tours of his former Mexican haunts. In other words, Rick is getting the message out by every means possible. In order to be able to render Mexico's cuisine so beautifully, Rick must have lived there in another lifetime. I don't think I would have traveled there if I had never met him.

Mesquite-Smoked Grilled Turkey with Red Chile-Adobo Sauce and Jicama-Cranberry Relish

Makes 10 to 12 servings

For the turkey
1 whole fresh turkey (12 to 14 pounds), well rinsed, giblets removed
2 gallons water
1 cup packed dark brown sugar
1 cup salt
1 tablespoon crushed red pepper flakes
2 cups mesquite wood chips
6 garlic cloves, crushed
1 bunch fresh marjoram
  OR
1 tablespoon dried marjoram
1 bunch fresh thyme
  OR
1 tablespoon dried thyme
10 to 12 bay leaves
  Vegetable oil, for brushing on turkey

To brine the turkey: If the turkey has a metal clamp on its legs, remove and discard it. Line a large, clean dishpan or plastic bucket, deep enough to submerge your turkey with a double layer of food-safe plastic bags. (I like Reynolds turkey-roasting bags.) Add 1 gallon of the water, the sugar, salt, and crushed pepper. Stir the mixture to dissolve the sugar and salt, then add the remaining gallon of water and mix. Place the turkey in the brine, breast side down, making sure it is completely submerged. Squeeze the air out of the bags and tie them shut. Refrigerate 12 hours or overnight.

To set up the grill for indirect cooking: Soak the wood chips in water to cover for at least 30 minutes. Heat a gas grill to medium-high, or light a charcoal fire and let it burn just until the coals are covered with gray ash and it's very hot.

When the grill is ready, either turn the burner(s) in the center to medium-low or bank the coals to the sides for indirect cooking. Add some of the soaked wood chips to the grill. (If you're using a gas grill, place the wood chips in a smoker attachment box or wrap them in foil and place them in the grill. (If you're using a charcoal grill, place the wood chips directly on the hot coals then position the grill grate on top.)

To prepare the turkey for the grill: In the meantime, remove the turkey from the brine and pat thoroughly dry with paper towels. (If you are not cooking the turkey at this point, transfer it to the outer roasting bag, which should still be dry and clean, and refrigerate, discarding the brine.) Rub the inside of the turkey cavity with the crushed garlic, stuff the herbs inside, then tie the legs together with a cotton string. Pull the skin over the neck opening and secure it with a small skewer. Place the turkey, breast side up, on a roasting rack set inside a heavy-gauge foil pan. Brush the turkey lightly with the vegetable oil.

To grill the turkey: Pour 1 cup water over the grill then set the turkey in the pan on the cooking grate. Cover the grill and cook the turkey over medium heat; estimate 12 to 14 minutes per pound, typically 2½ to 3 hours total. To maintain an even temperature with a charcoal grill, add more charcoal regularly (a few pieces every half hour or so). Keep adding wood chips for desired smokiness.

Check the turkey periodically; you may want to cover the wing tips or the whole turkey to prevent the skin from getting too brown. The turkey is done when its juices run clear and the internal temperature of the thickest part of the thigh is about 170°F. When it is cooked, remove the turkey from the grill, cover loosely with foil, and let stand 15 minutes. (The temperature will rise 5 to 10 degrees as the turkey rests.)

Carve the turkey, arrange the meat on a warm platter, and serve it with the warm Red Chile-Adobo Sauce and the Jicama-Cranberry Relish (recipes below).

For the chile sauce
⅓ cup vegetable oil
12 dried ancho chiles, (about 6 ounces total) stemmed, seeded, and torn into flat pieces
6 garlic cloves, roughly chopped
2 teaspoons dried oregano, preferably Mexican
1 teaspoon freshly ground pepper

½ teaspoon cumin, preferably freshly ground
¼ teaspoon cloves, preferably freshly ground
½ cup cider vinegar
4 cups turkey or chicken broth (I like to use the turkey neck and giblets to make the broth)
Salt
2 to 3 tablespoons sugar

Measure the vegetable oil into a large skillet over medium heat. When the oil is hot, toast the chiles, 1 or 2 pieces at a time for a few seconds per side, until they are very fragrant and blistered. Pour off all but a generous film of oil from the skillet and set aside. Transfer the toasted chiles to a large bowl and cover with 4 cups hot tap water; a small plate positioned on top will keep the chiles submerged. Let them rehydrate for about 20 minutes.

Measure the garlic, oregano, pepper, cumin, cloves, and vinegar into a blender or food processor. Pour in the rehydrated chiles, liquid and all (do this in two batches if necessary), then process the mixture to a smooth purée. Press the purée through a medium-mesh strainer set over a bowl.

Set the skillet used to toast the chiles over medium heat. When quite hot, add the adobo puree and stir until it's reduced to the thickness of tomato paste, about 10 minutes. Stir in the broth, reduce the heat to medium-low, and simmer for 30 minutes. Although the finished sauce should not be watery, it should be quite light in texture. (A good test is to pour a little of the sauce on a plate and watch it spread: if it flows evenly, it's done. If it doesn't flow much and water separates from around the edges, the sauce is too thick.) Season with salt (usually about 1 tablespoon) and the sugar; the sauce should be a little sweet-sour with a hint of saltiness. Serve warm. The finished sauce will keep for days if refrigerated in an air tight container.

For the relish
1 large red onion, finely diced
1½ cups jicama, finely diced
½ cup chopped dried cranberries (unsweetened)
3 tablespoons cider vinegar
Salt
6 tablespoons coarsely chopped fresh cilantro

Combine the onion, jicama, dried cranberries, and vinegar. Taste and season with a little salt, then stir in the cilantro. This relish is best made within a couple hours of dinner.

Norman Van Aken

Each year *Bon Appétit* magazine hosts both the American Food and Entertaining Awards in various American cities. Whether they're from the East or West Coast or the hottest thing in the South, all the celebrity chefs come together under one roof for these events to offer samples of their creations. It's quite a scene. Wineries from all across the world offer their best vintages, and connoisseurs move from station to station to taste which creations best compliment their Merlot or Chardonnay. Everyone has little platefuls of tuna tartar or scallops topped with caviar, and a lot of wine. Just like certain amusement park rides, several chefs have very long lines because the adventurous guests insist on their turn at the table. One night in Miami in 1997, Norman Van Aken's line was the longest, because his food is worth the wait.

Until then I'd only heard about the Florida-based chef who had invented something called New World Cuisine. The term "fusion" had been tossed around for some time, but I didn't understand exactly what it meant until Norman broke it down for me. His cooking springs from the flavors and dishes of Key West and its parent cultures, including both the Old World (Spain, the Mediterranean Basin, Africa) and the New World (Cuba, the Caribbean, the North American Southwest, Latin America). This, along with a touch of Asian and Cajun, is the palette Norman draws upon. Using both folk and classical cooking methods, he juxtaposes tropical South Florida ingredients like conch, mango, coconut, key lime, and grouper with what he calls "crossover flavors" (mainly spices) to create New World Cuisine. Norman's food does justice to each of the cuisines he borrows from, while creating something new and wonderful in the process. It sounds complicated because it is, and nobody else could have pulled it off. There was certainly no tuna tartar at Norman's booth at the benefit: he was serving achiote-marinated skewered quail with torn greens and papaya chili.

Born in Diamond Lake, Illinois, Norman felt as though Key West was the pot of gold at the end of the rainbow. However, his culinary journey was not without a few detours. After dropping out of college, he traveled around the country, working as a short-order cook in various places along his route. In 1973 Norman arrived in Key West, where, for a decade he read cookbooks, compared notes with other cooks, and researched the regional cuisines. He didn't just prepare Cuban black beans and plantains, he investigated the roots of the dish: the exact spices used when it was first introduced into Cuba, where the people of the region originated, and what traditions influenced their way of cooking.

Because Norman is self-taught, it's all the more impressive that he had the courage to come on the scene and claim, "I have something new to offer the world." After all, diners know what to expect from a French chef; they have standard dishes against which to measure his fare. But Norman's ambition was to create a cuisine where none had existed before, taking a considerable risk before a highly critical audience.

Norman coined the term "fusion" and earned a reputation as a chef at South Florida's legendary Louie's Backyard and the cutting-edge a Mano. He practiced, he tested, and he dreamed of bringing the flavors of all these places together. He made his recipes available in a cookbook called *Feast of Sunlight*, and on the basis of its success was able to gather a small group to invest half a million dollars in a restaurant of his own. When Norman's opened in the Miami neighborhood of Coral Gables in 1995, it put the South Florida food scene on the map. Norman stands in conscious opposition to the homogenization of American food and the generic dishes that characterized the food of Florida (and many other places). He wants to see ethnic treats such as empanadas and spring rolls at the grocery store along with the staples of mainstream American fare. He believes that no cuisine in the world is inherently superior to any other; it's the amazing regional variations that inspire him.

From the beginning, the Miami restaurant was a huge hit. There was so much hype about the mysterious New World Cuisine that Norman's soon became a destination for serious foodies, who would plan their trips to Florida around a meal there. As the buzz grew, Norman began to explain what he was doing. When you walk into the restaurant for the first time, you can tell it's built around a certain philosophy. His kitchen is a very serious environment, with the sous-chef, line cooks, and waiters well versed in New World Cuisine and aware of its importance.

For Norman, "fusion" also means combining rustic traditions with those of haute cuisine. In the Cuban dish Pork Havana, the meat is usually marinated for a day in seasonings such as sour oranges, garlic, onions, and pepper and then roasted to the point where the meat is falling off the bone. In Cuba, it would be served with plantains, black beans, and yellow rice. Norman marinates and roasts the pork in the same way, but in his hands it becomes Pork Havana Nuevo, meaning "new style." He omits the rice and beans and serves it with fried plantains. And he creates a new element by integrating the traditional black beans into a black bean sauce. A dish like his Criolla Mama Barbecue Shrimp with Corn and Goat Cheese Torta mingles the flavors of the Southwest and the Yucatán with a touch of New Orleans.

Like actors, some chefs have high-profile years and then aren't heard from for a year or two, but people are always talking about Norman. Rather than taking his success for granted, he constantly works to redefine his art. A respected writer, he lectures internationally about New World Cuisine and is one of the only American chefs to have won the James Beard Award, the Robert Mondavi Award, and the Food Arts Silver Spoon. His cookbooks have also won awards, and though not everyone would attempt to duplicate his complex dishes at home, the books are a valuable resource to learn about Norman's New World Cuisine.

If all the chefs in this book got together in one room, they wouldn't agree on where to get the finest duck or who manufactures the best sauté pan. But they would all say that Norman is a genius and that they'd learned from him in some way. Norman's cooking shows the value of taking a chance, going out on a limb, expecting the unexpected.

Chocolate Gooey Cake

Makes 8 to 10 servings

$1\frac{1}{4}$ cups sugar
  1 tablespoon unsalted butter, plus more for pan
$\frac{1}{2}$ cup heavy cream
  1 cup flour, plus more for pan
$\frac{1}{4}$ teaspoon salt
  1 teaspoon baking powder
$5\frac{1}{2}$ tablespoons cocoa powder
  1 cup pecans, chopped
$\frac{1}{2}$ cup packed brown sugar
$1\frac{1}{4}$ cups hot coffee

Preheat the oven to 350°F. Butter and flour a large, glass loaf pan and set aside.

In an electric mixer, cream $\frac{3}{4}$ cup of the sugar with the butter. Add the cream, flour, salt, baking powder, and $1\frac{1}{2}$ tablespoons of the cocoa. Rub some butter on your hands and spread the batter in the cake pan.

In a separate bowl, combine the remaining $\frac{1}{2}$ cup sugar, the pecans and brown sugar, and the remaining 4 tablespoons cocoa. Sprinkle this topping over the batter, then pour the coffee over the entire cake and bake for 1 hour.

Scoop out portions of the cake with a large spoon and serve warm with the very best vanilla ice cream.

Sara Moulton

Sara Moulton joined the Food Network in the fall of 1995 to do an hour-long show called "Cooking Live," which was the first interactive cooking show on television. Viewers could call in with questions about the dish Sara was making or ask completely unrelated cooking queries. The producers would then relay these questions to Sara through an ear-piece. As soon as the show went on the air, the phone lines lit up. Hosting a show like this was not an easy task, but Sara can field any kind of question like a pro, come up with the answer, and keep the show moving. She's quick on her feet and very serious about teaching people about the food that means so much to her.

Sara single-handedly revolutionized the way consumers could get information on demand about products, menus, and techniques, and "Cooking Live" was an instant hit. A lot of Sara's ratings come from her forthrightness. When she doesn't know something, instead of fumbling through she'll say, "You got me. I'm going to look that one up, and if I can't get to you later in the show, tune in tomorrow." The audience has turned into her collaborator, often calling in with answers or suggestions such as reducing the number of eggs in an upside-down cake. When mistakes happen, her attitude is always, "Don't panic. Take control of the situation, don't let the situation control you."

Sara loves to teach real cooking to real people, whether they're working moms, single dads, or college kids boiling water for the first time. She provides sensible alternatives to burgers and fries with quick tips for making a ham or pot roast and why to swap those cans on the shelf for fresh vegetables. She might feature an Easter dinner that isn't intimidating, or suggest something special for an anniversary or other special occasion—a crown roast stuffed with sage and sausage. "Cooking Live" was almost like a televised lifestyle magazine; you could leaf through it for ideas and take what you wanted. Sara's a great liaison to average Americans who didn't grow up cooking next to their grandmothers but who enjoy good food and want to be creative.

Sara is currently doing another show for the Food Network called "Sara's Secrets." Each thirty-minute show gives viewers a one-to-one taste of Sara as she lets them in on the shortcuts, insider tips, and secrets that make them come out of the kitchen looking like culinary geniuses. More entertainment-oriented, the show encourages viewers to cook for friends over the weekend and to feel capable and comfortable in their own kitchen, even if they're not accomplished chefs.

Sara is much more than a television chef, however. She graduated with the highest honors from the Culinary Institute of America in 1977, after which she went to work at the Harvest, located in Cambridge, Massachusetts, celebrated for its regional American fare. While in Boston, she started working behind the scenes as an associate chef on Julia Child's PBS series "Julia Child and More Company." Sara and Julia developed a strong working relationship, and Julia suggested that Sara apprentice in France, where she cooked with master chef Maurice Cazalis in his one-star restaurant one hour south of Paris in the town of Chartres. Upon her return to Boston, Sara cooked at Cybele's, where dishes like slow roasted duck, earned the restaurant a good review from the *Boston Globe*. In 1981 Sara returned to her hometown, New York City, to take a position at Cafe New Amsterdam, eventually leaving there for a position as *chef tournant* at La Tulipe. *Chef tournant* means "rounds cook"—preparing sauces one day, appetizers the next, salads the third, and so on—and on Sundays she took on the chef's job. It turned out to be the best experience imaginable for Sara because of the various roles she had to master.

A lot of people in the culinary world don't talk about its sexism, but the industry is male-dominated. One of the first to say enough is enough, Sara cofounded an organization in 1982 called the New York Women's Culinary Alliance, a group of female culinary professionals who network and promote the advancement of women in the business. Its existence alone has been a much-needed wake-up call to the industry.

Sara's career took a new turn when she began teaching cooking classes at Peter Kump's New York Cooking School from 1983 to 1985. She also began working at *Gourmet* magazine in 1984, rising to the position of executive chef four years later. At *Gourmet* Sara is in charge of the executive dining room, cooking for the magazine's advertisers and important clients. She runs it just like a restaurant kitchen, serving up everything from Korean beef with a soba noodle salad to lamb with couscous. Sara loves the fact that in this job she can be as creative as she wants, and she impresses diners with her ability to make the promise of *Gourmet's* pages come to life. If she's not cooking for high-powered guests, Sara often holds impromptu cooking classes, showing staffers how to julienne vegetables or the secret to frying coconut shrimp.

The transition from professional kitchen to teaching kitchen was a difficult one—Sara had assumed she'd spend her career in restaurants—but she realized that as a full-time educator she could reach many more people. That audience grew far larger when Sara appeared on "Good Morning America." Julia Child had brought her over to do the food preparation for her appearances on the show, and in 1987 the "Good Morning America" staff brought Sara aboard as the executive chef for all their food segments. If a guest cancelled or a cookbook author couldn't make it, Sara went on the air, and the audience loved her.

A lot of television personalities save their energy for when the camera rolls, but not Sara, who is far more involved in the day-to-day running of her show than many other chefs on television. Sara is very petite, but she makes it known from the beginning that she's in charge. She does a lot of the pre-planning and comes up with many of the the ideas that actually translate from script to television that her team then researches and develops. Ensuring that she's comfortable with the information presented on her show enables Sara to speak with an ease and authority that translates to the viewers at home.

Sara gets more done in one day than most people accomplish in a week. Married to a music industry guru who ran his own record label and now consults on various music projects, she's up by 6 A.M. to get her kids, Ruth, fifteen, and Sam, twelve, ready for school. She's in her office at *Gourmet* by nine o'clock, and, when she was doing "Cooking Live," was there until a car picked her up at 5 P.M. to whisk her across town to the Food Network to prep for the show. You might not have seen Sara when she came in, but you'd hear her voice—she would be bouncing off the walls with energy for her live show. She headed for the little "pod" where her culinary producers were waiting for any changes on the script they faxed her earlier in the day. Before you knew it she'd changed from her *Gourmet* gear into a standard-cut but brightly colored chef's jacket, with a pair of hi-top Converse sneakers that usually matched. She didn't go in for a lot of make-up or big television hair, instead she just put it up in a simple ponytail or French twist. Sara didn't waste a minute once she got into "the zone"—a state of mental and physical preparedness—because with a live show there's no time buffer. When it's time, the cameras are rolling.

Sara carried the same energy she brought into the building down to the set. The network has a whole culinary team—executive chef, sous-chefs, buyers, prep cooks, choppers, dishwashers—that works like any restaurant crew. If Sara's menu that night featured gourmet burgers, she would check out the texture and quality of the meat, that everything she needs was laid out properly—it's called the *mise en place*—including the piece of Cheddar to stick in the middle of the burger as a cheese surprise for a picky eater in the family. She wants to show people the right way to do things, and on live television you only get one chance. Then she walked over to the set, greeted everyone on the crew by name—they're almost like extended family—got one last touch of make-up, went behind the stove, and at 6:59 P.M. she heard, "Five, four, three, two, one, you're on," and the adrenaline kicked in: "This is Sara Moulton. Thanks for joining me on 'Cooking Live.'"

People always ask what Sara is like in person. I say Sara is that girlfriend that we all have who doesn't take no for an answer. She's a great leader, an overachiever, her own worst critic, and a very compassionate person. Early in my career, a show I had started called "Recipes for Health" got cancelled. Rumors had been flying, and I knew it was coming, but I still took it hard. Sara was the only person who didn't avoid me on the day the news came down. I was surveying my puffy eyes under the gloomy fluorescent lighting in the ladies' room when Sara came in. Although she had her jacket on, make-up done, ready to go live in less than ten minutes, when I put my hand down on the counter she put hers on top of mine and assured me that everyone knew my value. Before leaving she helped me wipe my tears, and when I looked back in the mirror I felt ready to take control of the situation, Sara-style.

The bottom line is that Sara is many things. She's been nominated twice for the James Beard Award for Best National Television Show. In 2002 she was inducted into the James Beard Who's Who of Food and Beverage in America, one of the industry's most prestigious awards. Known as Julia Child's protégée she's received the Sara Lee Frontrunner Award, which honors women of remarkable accomplishment. Sara is a leader, a brilliant chef, and an important voice for women who want equality in the restaurant kitchen. Yet she's home every night in time to check homework, tuck the kids into bed, and spend some quality time with her husband, which is the most important part of her day.

Soft-Shell Crabs with Spicy Tartar Sauce

Makes 4 servings

For the sauce
1½ cups mayonnaise
⅜ cup finely chopped dill pickles
⅜ cup finely chopped red onion, soaked in ice water for 15 minutes, drained, and patted dry
3 tablespoons capers, rinsed, drained, and chopped
¼ cup chopped fresh cilantro
2 tablespoons fresh lime juice
½ to 1 chipotle chile pepper in adobo sauce, or to taste, minced
Salt and pepper

For the crabs
8 small soft-shell crabs, cleaned thoroughly
Whole milk, for soaking the crabs
1 cup Wondra flour or all-purpose flour
Salt and pepper
Vegetable oil, for sautéing
Lime wedges, for garnish

To make the tartar sauce: Stir all the sauce ingredients together and season with salt and pepper to taste. Cover and refrigerate while making the crabs.

To prepare the crabs: Place them in a bowl with just enough milk to cover them; cover and refrigerate for 30 minutes. When the crabs have finished soaking, season the flour with salt and pepper to taste and transfer it to a shallow pie dish lined with parchment paper. Working in batches, remove the crabs from the milk, letting the excess drip off, and dredge them in the flour mixture, lifting up the sides of the parchment paper to help coat the crabs evenly with the flour.

Add ¼-inch vegetable oil to a large skillet and heat over moderately high heat until almost smoking. Add the crabs to the skillet, shell side up first, and cook on both sides, about 3 minutes per side, until brown and crisp. Be careful—they splatter. As the crabs finish cooking, transfer them to a platter, shell side down, and cover loosely with foil to keep warm. Repeat the procedure with the remaining crabs.

Serve the crabs immediately, topping each portion with the tartar sauce and a lime wedge.

Matthew Kenney

Every year *Food & Wine* magazine puts out an August issue announcing the top new chefs in America. Foodies always make sure to pick up that issue, and in 1994 Matthew Kenney was in it. He was one of a few chefs chosen that year from New York City.

The article talked about his new restaurant on Manhattan's Upper East Side called Matthew's, which served Mediterranean food. It was nearly impossible to get a reservation after that article appeared, but a few weeks later three women friends and I showed up for dinner.

The place had an exotic feel, with enormous windows, tall palms, and low wicker seating—and while every single person who worked there was gorgeous, definitely a hand picked part of the experience, they knew their stuff. They explained the chef's take on each dish on the menu, and the way he had interpreted Mediterranean ingredients for the American palate, such as spiced crab cakes. Matthew is from Maine, where crab cakes are a standard, but he seasoned them with lemon, cumin, cardamom, and ginger, making them very spicy.

I had the crab cakes, and also the Moroccan spiced shrimp on sugar cane skewers—North African cuisine with a bit of a Caribbean touch. For dessert there was an array of options: flavored sorbets, a flourless chocolate torte, an almond cake soaked in almond milk served with a pudding of figs and dates (the chef's favorite), caramelized pineapple with rice pudding, and a port wine flan with pears and Roquefort crisps. At the end of the meal the maître d' saw us smiling and brought Matthew out to meet us. What a contrast with the poised, confident person in the *Food & Wine* photograph! Matthew was completely shy and self-effacing, reminding me of the cute guy in fifth grade who has no idea that all the girls have a crush on him. When we told him it was one of

the best, most refreshing meals we'd had in New York City, he thanked us and scooted back into the kitchen.

When it comes to presentation, Matthew cultivates a particular aesthetic for each of his seven restaurants, as well as at each event his company caters. At Matthew's, where the look is particularly airy and minimalist, he used only white plates so the strong colors and distinctive aromas of each dish came forward on their own. Minimalist, however, doesn't necessarily mean simple. Each course arrived on a plate of a distinct size and shape—some triangular, some irregular—that perfectly complimented the dish.

Matthew's food not only looks good, it's good for you, because Mediterranean food is naturally low-fat. He was one of the innovators of "Mediterranean Rim" cuisine, which encompasses not just the tastes of Southern France, Italy, and Greece, but extends through North Africa, Egypt, and Turkey. Instead of butter, salt, or heavy sauces, he relies on olive oil, fresh light ingredients, and aromatic herbs and spices. Matthew will take a piece of salmon, and instead of sautéing it or hiding it under a cream sauce, he'll roast it with fresh coriander and ginger. The luxurious flavors of almonds, apricots, and olives are layered throughout many of his dishes. They're not rich, but they're nonetheless indulgent to the palate!

About three months after I had dinner at Matthew's, David Rosengarten, the host of "In Food Today," wanted to do a show on Moroccan cuisines. At the pitch meeting I revealed I had the perfect guest—a little shy but loaded with potential. My qualifier made my colleagues nervous, but I figured that Matthew would get over his shyness and that his food would speak for him. David knew Matthew was serious about his food, so we booked the show.

Matthew was very quiet when he came into the studio, but he did a wonderful segment on how to marinate, season, and bake a lamb shank. He didn't just talk about cooking, he gave tips on how the butcher should cut the meat and what it should cost. Watching Matthew confirmed the truth of the adage that there is often more to people than first meets the eye.

Matthew found his calling almost by accident. After growing up in Searsport, Maine, he graduated from the University of Maine and was headed for law school when he came to New York City to visit a college friend. Since his friend loved to dine out, Matthew spent his stay visiting one little eatery after another and was captivated by the excitement and variety of the New York City restaurant scene. His parents weren't too pleased when he announced his intention to trade in the law books for a chef's toque, but they must have felt better when he graduated from New York's French Culinary Institute in 1990, and then received the school's Outstanding Alumnus Award in 1995.

Matthew was inspired by extensive travel in Egypt, Turkey, Greece, Spain, Italy, France, and Morocco. He found the techniques and ingredients of these regional cuisines healthier than the traditional preparations taught at the French Culinary Institute, and it was these non-traditional tastes that helped him carve out a niche in the New York fine dining scene. After graduating, Matthew came up with the idea of a restaurant that served Moroccan food. He'd been getting very good reviews as the chef at a restaurant called Alo Alo until the night a taxi crashed through the front window, requiring the restaurant to close for repair. Matthew approached the owners about re-opening it as his own Mediterranean place, and the doors to Matthew's opened in 1994.

His second restaurant, named Mezze, featured Mediterranean food in a less formal setting. A hallmark was the use of flatbreads for pizza and sandwiches, a more portable version of Mediterranean for the Midtown business lunch crowd. Matthew then opened Monzu in Soho, focusing on Sicilian food, specifically the style that was influenced by the French chefs Napoleon brought to Sicily. While Monzu opened to great critical acclaim, the food and atmosphere proved to be a little too esoteric for the trendy younger downtown crowd. After two years, Matthew decided to change the concept and opened Canteen in 1999. Canteen serves American bistro fare in a retro-modern setting, with a menu characterized by Matthew's layering of savory spices to bring out natural flavors. He serves sea bass with bok choy, and sautéed spinach alongside sinful truffled macaroni and cheese. Then came the hip eatery, Commune, in the Flatiron District.

In the middle of this expansion, a terrible kitchen fire closed Matthew's down overnight. Instead of rebuilding it as the original Matthew's he turned the original Upper East Side space into yet another restaurant, called Commissary. Well aware that his old clientele would be watching closely, Mathew hired the design team of David and Eve-Lynn Schefer and architect Richard Lewis, and retained two chefs, Larry Kolar, who is also currently the chef at Commune, and Sarma Melngailis. Sarma had left investment banking to attend the French Culinary Institute when she met Matthew at his namesake restaurant—the one she'd chosen for her wedding shower. Over a year later, they met again to begin collaborating on a new cookbook. It was not long before the two ended up separating from their respective spouses, falling in love, and moving in together. Knowing Matthew's tastes well, Sarma wooed him with a salad of arugula with manchego, roasted almonds, and quince dressing. This and many other recipes for Commissary's opening menu were developed during a summer they spent in a cottage on the ocean in Searsport, Maine, the town where Matthew grew up. Instead of specializing in a single cuisine, the menu capitalizes on the skills of all three chefs and features dishes chosen from all over the world. Matthew has since expanded his empire to include a second Commissary in Portland, Maine, and taken over the historic Nickerson Tavern in Searsport. In keeping with his emphasis on artful seasoning, Matthew's Maine dishes take full advantage of local flavors like pumpkin, fiddle-head ferns, maple syrup, and of course, lobster.

Matthew's restaurants look very different from one another, and the menus are fairly diverse. But each is enormously sophisticated and has succeeded with its target audience. The uptown crowd, which wants formal, complex dishes, might go for pistachio and anise-crusted halibut with honey and lemon sauce, while downtowners can stop into Canteen for a full-flavored chicken potpie. Whether or not the cuisine is fancy, if Matthew's name is attached to a restaurant, people come there for the ambience and general sensibility. As the proprietor of restaurants that are often compared to nightclubs, he has a knack for what's been called "scene cuisine"—a place not just to eat but to see and be seen.

Matthew is the only chef I know who meditates. He does yoga, and feels his best strategizing in Central Park or the Union Square greenmarket, with a little distance from the kitchen. Matthew has evolved from chef to chef/restaurateur. He's found a way to turn his culinary skills into an entrepreneurial dream, and he's still spreading his wings.

Roasted Lamb Loin Stuffed with Almonds, Dates, Goat Cheese, and Mint

Makes 6 servings

¾ cup almonds
2 lamb loins (about 10 ounces each), trimmed but with a thin layer of fat remaining
   Kosher salt and freshly ground pepper
2 ounces soft goat cheese
½ cup pitted, coarsely chopped dates
2 tablespoons coarsely chopped or torn fresh mint leaves
4 tablespoons olive oil
½ cup fresh orange juice (from 2 medium oranges)
2 tablespoons honey
½ cup loosely packed fresh cilantro, leaves only

Preheat the oven to 350°F. Place the almonds on a baking sheet and toast until golden and fragrant, about 10 minutes. Coarsely chop and set aside.

Increase oven temperature to 400°F. Place each lamb loin between two sheets of plastic wrap and, using a meat mallet, pound to about ¾-inch thickness. (If you don't have a meat mallet, the flat bottom of a glass bottle or the side of a wine bottle should work well, but use caution so you don't break the bottle.)

Lay one of the pounded lamb loins on a flat work surface. Season with salt and pepper. Spread the goat cheese on top, leaving a ½-inch border all around. Top with the mint and about half the chopped almonds and dates; reserve the rest for garnish. Season the other lamb loin with salt and pepper and place, seasoned side down, on top of the first loin, matching the edges as much as possible so the filling will not come out. Tightly tie the lamb loins crosswise with kitchen twine. Season all over with more salt and pepper.

Heat 2 tablespoons of the olive oil in a large, ovenproof skillet over medium-high heat. When the oil is hot, sear the lamb loins, rotating as each side is seared, 1 to 2 minutes per side. Place the skillet in the oven and roast the lamb, 6 to 8 minutes for medium rare. Remove from the oven and allow to rest, about 10 minutes.

Meanwhile, to make the vinaigrette, combine the orange juice, honey, and cilantro in a nonreactive bowl. Whisk in the 2 remaining tablespoons oil, adding it in a steady stream. Season with salt and pepper.

To serve, cut away the twine and discard. Carefully slice the stacked lamb loins into ¾-inch-thick slices. Fan the slices on individual plates or on a serving platter. Spoon the vinaigrette over and around the lamb and sprinkle with the remaining chopped almonds and dates.

Leah Chase

When foodies travel, they recommend memorable restaurants to each other. In 1997 my fiancé and I were heading to New Orleans. My good friend, the chef Marcus Samuelsson, had recently attended a Black Culinary Alliance Dinner in New York City honoring Leah Chase. He said, "Go to Dooky Chase and tell Leah I sent you."

We were staying at the Windsor Court, an elegant downtown hotel. When we told the bellman where we were headed, he said, "Oh, you're in for a treat, 'cause she makes some mean food!" The concierge seconded that opinion, adding, "Make sure you get a cab back home too." And then the cabby put in his two cents worth, "Have the gumbo." So we definitely felt like we were on the right track. As we approached the restaurant, we understood the concierge's advice. We were on the outskirts of the city, in a neighborhood marked by abandoned buildings and deep poverty. But sitting on the corner was an old building with the original black-and-white sign hanging outside, announcing that you'd arrived at Dooky Chase.

Leah married into the business when she wed Edgar Dooky Chase III, a well known New Orleans musician. She lets you know right off the bat, however, that her husband can't boil water: "He pays the bills and I run the house." Her in-laws owned the Globe Sandwich Shop, which opened across the street from the present location in 1939. Leah came onboard when they moved to the present location and renamed the restaurant after Leah's father-in-law. After sixty-three years, the partnership is still going strong. Leah was never formally trained—she just got into the kitchen and started cooking. Finding that she liked being in charge of the kitchen, she took local cooking courses to learn more about her native Creole cuisine.

The restaurant is far from fancy, but it has its own funky style: bright pink walls, glass-topped pink tablecloths, and chairs that look like they belong in a bingo hall. It reminded me of the comforting places of my childhood where the black community socialized. The waiters are young kids from the neighborhood, but what they lack in expertise they make up for in hospitality. And Dooky Chase has some surprises. There's gorgeous art on the walls by talented African-Americans complete with a sign describing the artists and listing prices of the work, so the restaurant also functions as a little gallery. And the diversity of the crowd left my mouth hanging open—young white kids and middle-aged Asian couples; locals and tourists; a lot of mixed tables. You forget you're off the beaten track in a dicey neighborhood once you're inside.

The restaurant has about one hundred and fifty covers (a table in the restaurant business is called a cover), while the kitchen is only the size of a closet. It could be Leah's own kitchen at home, and she is hands-on, literally hovering over every pot. You better know that she made that jambalaya, trimmed the sausage, peeled the shrimp, and cleaned the okra. The food is served on regular commercial china, but it's delicious and comforting, and that's why all kinds of people keep coming back to Dooky Chase.

Gumbo is one of Leah's signature dishes. The way she can add flavor sets it apart, and I don't think it's teachable. She'd talk about her secret ingredients—chicken necks, hard-shell crabs, smoked sausages, shrimp, chicken gizzards, chicken wings, and veal stew meat—but when it came to the spices, she laughed, "Girl, there are some secrets that are just between me and God, and this is one of them." The only thing she revealed is that "It's all in the filé powder." Filé, a seasoning made from the ground dried leaves of the sassafras tree, is an essential ingredient of gumbo and a number of other Creole dishes. (The choosiest chefs in New Orleans buy theirs from Lionel Key, whose family has been making filé for over twenty-five years.)

Timing in seasoning is everything, so there's also enormous skill involved in when Leah adds the spices. Over the course of the day, while the cooks are prepping, she's constantly testing with her teaspoon, making sure the dishes are perfect. Another great dish is her shrimp remoulade. This is a classic Creole dish available all over New Orleans. It looks like shrimp cocktail, but instead of cocktail sauce, it's served with remoulade: a mayonnaise-based sauce seasoned with Creole spices. The texture of it is so wonderful that the shrimp almost feels like an afterthought.

You can get jambalaya at the corner stores too, but Leah's huge portions show off all the ingredients—big chunks of chicken, andouille, and other Creole hot sausages. When you see what you get, you realize it's more than your money's worth. There's nothing skimpy about Leah's food. And of course she makes the classic fried chicken and catfish, dipped in cornmeal she spices in her own special way, blackened and fried to a crisp. Her stuffed crabs, two little blue crabs to a serving, are incredible. You can taste their freshness, and they're stuffed with shrimp, sausage, vegetables, lobster, fish, and of course the crabmeat. As for the desserts, there are probably several pounds of butter in Leah's pound cake. As my grandmother would say, "This cake is so good it'll make you want to slap your mother." The Bananas Foster, a banana cake served with a little whipped cream and decadent milk chocolate drizzled on top is another favorite.

It's not unusual for Leah to join people at the table for dessert. If the plate isn't cleaned, she'll ask, "Is something wrong?" I've seen her go so far as to tell a very slender diner, who happened to be my guest, "Girl, don't bring that 'I'll just have a salad,' or 'I'm on a diet' mentality down here. If you're in New Orleans, you've got to eat!" Leah has sixteen grandchildren and four great-grandchildren, and when we're at her restaurant we're all her children.

The atmosphere makes Dooky Chase the perfect place for people who want to feel like they're eating in a New Orleans home. The personalized attention that Leah gives everybody— the mayor happened to be there that night, but it wasn't just his table or mine that she visited—makes eating there as close to home cooking as possible. Meals have the feeling of a Sunday dinner, a time to get together and catch up. Leah doesn't use measuring cups, and she isn't trying to re-create a recipe from a cookbook. She's cooking with her heart and soul. Although she's happy doing what she does, you can tell from her face that things didn't always come easy.

Leah grew up when the South was highly segregated. When she took over the restaurant, it was the local joint, with a mostly African-American clientele. She worked hard to bring her family and her husband's family's history, the dishes she grew up with, to a larger audience. She didn't need to get fancy or reinvent the wheel. By preserving authentic Creole and keeping the recipes true, the world found her. Celebrities like Count Basie, Sarah Vaughan, Lena Horne, and John F. Kennedy have all frequented Dooky Chase's, and, like Leah herself, it's become a local institution. She's the queen of Creole cooking in New Orleans, and the title is well deserved.

Green Tomato Casserole

Makes 6 servings

- 6 large green tomatoes (2½ to 3 pounds), cored and sliced
- ¼ cup unsalted butter or vegetable oil
- 3 cups seasoned dry breadcrumbs
- 1 cup chopped green onions
- ¼ cup chopped fresh parsley
- 3 large eggs, beaten
- ¼ pound Cheddar cheese, shredded (1 cup)
- ¼ pound Romano, shredded (1 cup)
- one 12-ounce can evaporated milk
- 1 teaspoon pepper
- 1 teaspoon salt

Thoroughly grease a Pyrex baking dish with the butter or vegetable oil. Preheat the oven to 400°F.

Mix 2 cups of the breadcrumbs with the onions, parsley, and one beaten egg. Set aside. Combine the two cheeses and set aside.

Place a layer of tomatoes in the baking dish to cover the bottom of the dish. Spread the breadcrumb mixture over the tomatoes, then sprinkle half the cheese mixture on top of that. Cover with the remaining tomatoes.

Beat together the milk, salt, pepper, and two remaining eggs and pour the mixture over the casserole. Top with the remaining cheese and 1 cup remaining breadcrumbs.

Bake for 20 minutes, or until the casserole sets. Let cool a little, then cut in squares and serve warm.

Todd English

There's nothing wrong with a chef looking good, and none looks better than Todd English. He's over six feet tall, with dark hair, olive skin, and a Colgate smile that says "Trust me— I love food and sharing it with you is my great pleasure." Todd also likes to dress well. When they attend the cooking awards shows, most chefs probably pick out their attire that morning, but Todd starts thinking about a suit well ahead of time. Maybe Armani, perfectly cut, with a tie that makes a sophisticated statement will be his choice—nothing loud, or covered with chili peppers.

Though Todd and I first met at the 1994 James Beard Awards, his clothes aren't what I remember about that encounter. I'd already read a lot in newspapers and magazine about this young man from Boston whose food was becoming the talk of the town. The restaurant that brought him to my attention was called Figs and I remember reading about his gourmet pizza. It wasn't the typical anchovy or sausage pizza slathered with red sauce. In his toppings he used simply prepared fine ingredients in unexpected combinations, like roasted duck and goat cheese, white clams and portobellos, prosciutto and figs, arugula salad, or crispy onion rings.

That night Todd was named Best Chef in the Northeast Region. After winning that kind of award, you step up into the ranks of culinary royalty. People don't know that your sous-chef quit two days earlier and you haven't been to bed in thirty-six hours. Most winners walk around holding their award in front of them like a billboard, but Todd was cradling it in his arm, close to his heart. He looked like a man holding his baby for the first time, aware that something magical has happened. Todd had worked hard and he was really excited about the prestigious recognition.

Todd has a gentle way of speaking and an approachable manner that makes it easy to ask questions like, "Todd can you tell me why you have so many ingredients in your chestnut ravioli?" Todd's approach is to take simple, even common, foodstuffs and layer their tastes and textures into a complex whole. I've directed many people to Olives, Todd's outposts of Mediterranean restaurants. They'll take a look at the menu and say, "There's an awful lot going on in one dish." But when they come back, they say, "You were right. I'd never think to put venison in ravioli, but the meal was out of this world." Todd breaks the rules, and he gets away with it.

Todd started as a dishwasher in a little Mexican restaurant in Branford, Connecticut. By age seventeen he was a cook, but he also loved baseball and was talented enough to be offered a college scholarship by a Triple A league in Florida. His father dreamed of his son playing professional baseball, but instead

Todd heard another calling and chose the Culinary Institute of America, the Harvard of cooking schools. The CIA is very hard to get into: there's a rigorous academic curriculum, and it's known for training the best in the business. After graduating with honors, Todd could have written his ticket to any restaurant, but he didn't want to do someone else's food in someone else's restaurant. He had to find the kind of food that was right for him. Todd's mother is Italian, and he wanted to seek out a personal connection to this heritage, so he decided to apprentice in Italy's Piedmont region for two years.

He returned having mastered classic Piedmontese techniques and food combinations, but he gave them his own personal touch. Todd describes his food as his interpretation of Mediterranean cuisine, and in 1989 he opened up a restaurant in Boston called Olives that served this rustic Mediterranean food. Todd's signature dish is an olive tart made of marinated olives with goat cheese, caramelized onions, and anchovies in a pastry crust. The other dish he's known for is his tortelli of butternut squash with brown butter, sage, and Parmesan. He isn't redoing classical dishes with a new twist—he's experimenting. He's a food scientist, and he's not afraid to be adventurous.

Another specialty is Todd's Parmesan pudding, which is garnished with pea tendrils and mascarpone cream. He's also known for one of the best hollandaise sauces around. He makes a pan-seared wild king salmon, served over polenta with baby French asparagus, morels, and a crab hollandaise. Another of his signature dishes is a veal breast rolled and stuffed with prosciutto, duck confit, garlic and herbed potatoes served with a porcini gravy, peach chutney and a foie gras cream. You know a dish like that is going to taste extraordinary because the ingredients are so delicious, and it really does. Even when Todd combines unlikely elements, they work together.

Some chefs, like Wolfgang Puck or Emeril Lagasse, become famous very quickly. Others never become celebrities. For Todd, it didn't happen overnight, but he surrounded himself with a great team and had a vision. Within a year, thanks to word of mouth alone, his fifty-seat storefront restaurant, Olives, had people waiting in line for a taste of the Todd English experience. After winning the Best Chef award in 1994, he and his team went full-speed ahead. Over the next eight years, they opened up Olives in Las Vegas, Washington, D.C., Aspen, and New York. Figs branched out to five locations in Massachusetts and one in New York's LaGuardia Airport. Todd even consulted on a kosher Moroccan restaurant called Tamarind located in Eilat, Israel. He has live video feeds from each establishment into his Boston office so he can oversee the quality of the cooking and the service.

Todd is more than a chef: he's a public figure and a national brand, with his name on dozens of enterprises associated with rustic elegance. He markets food products, teaches wine pairings and one-on-one cooking lessons, and has plans to open a cooking school. He brilliantly capitalized on the growing trend to market not just remarkable restaurants but the chefs behind them. Todd and his team haven't lost the emphasis on first-rate food, but they've also excelled at franchising and building upon the English name, taking advantage of new media and the growing popular interest in cooking to shape a remarkable career.

Todd is committed to charities outside the culinary world and makes it his business to go directly into the community to support certain causes. Along with charities such as Share Our Strength, a New York-based fundraiser for the homeless and homebound, he's active with the Big Brother mentoring program and the Boys and Girls Club. He didn't just randomly pick the Boston Boys and Girls Club off a list, he's helping to rebuild the kitchen of the Charlestown location. He shows them simple dishes, demonstrates safe techniques, and lets them know that there's a fulfilling career in the cooking world beyond fast food and dishwashing. He tells them that if you love food, if it's a keen interest, you should follow your heart. That's his life, and he wants others to live out their dreams too.

Bay Scallops with Hazelnuts and Oranges

Makes 6 appetizer servings

¼ cup chestnut flour or other nut flour (all-purpose flour will do)
3 teaspoons kosher salt
¼ teaspoon freshly ground pepper, plus 1 to 2 teaspoons to taste
1 pound bay scallops, side muscles removed and discarded
2 tablespoons olive oil
3 tablespoons unsalted butter
1 medium shallot, minced
½ cup roughly chopped hazelnuts
1 dried chile pepper, minced
1 tablespoon chopped fresh thyme
1 tablespoon chopped fresh Italian parsley
½ cup fresh orange juice
½ cup chicken or veal stock
1 medium orange, seeds and membranes removed and discarded

In a small bowl, mix together the flour, 1 teaspoon of the salt and the ¼ teaspoon pepper. Add the scallops and toss lightly to coat. Gently scoop the scallops out of the flour and shake off any excess.

Heat a large nonstick skillet over medium-high and add the olive oil and 1 tablespoon of the butter. When the butter is melted, add the scallops and cook until they are deeply browned on all sides, 2 to 3 minutes. Transfer the scallops to a plate with a slotted spoon and set aside.

Wipe the skillet clean, then melt the remaining 2 tablespoons butter over medium heat. Add the shallot, hazelnuts, chile pepper, thyme, and parsley and cook, stirring occasionally, until the nuts are lightly browned, about 2 minutes. Add the orange juice and stock and raise the heat to thicken and reduce the liquid by half.

Add the orange segments, return the scallops to the skillet, and cook for 1 minute, tossing to combine. Season with the remaining 2 teaspoons salt and 1 to 2 teaspoons pepper. Spoon onto a large serving platter and serve immediately.

Bobby Flay

Bobby Flay is the bad boy of the food world. He's the quintessential celebrity chef, because he has just as much fun with the celebrity aspect as with being a chef. Not that he looks the part; with his freckles and red hair, Bobby comes across more like the all-American kid next door. He's from Generation X and more informal than many of his celebrity peers, yet he's one of the five most recognizable names in American cuisine today. If he gets out of a taxi, people call, "Hey Bobby, Bobby!" because they've seen him on television. He can't walk down a street in the Hamptons, which includes some of Long Island's most fashionable beach towns, without being approached by fans. Yet he's also the chef I'm most likely to spot across from me on the New York City subway.

I often run into Bobby at various parties on the nights of food awards or charity events. Half the room is asking where he's going next, because that's where the best party will be. He is the most chic chef on the circuit because he gives the impression that for him, every day is a party. I've never heard a chef describe his food as playful but it's true of Bobby's cooking. He made his mark with southwestern dishes that have very bold flavors and make brilliant use of chiles and spices. It's vibrant food, full of the charisma and spirit that make him so much fun to be with.

A native New Yorker, Bobby got his first restaurant job when he was seventeen, at the New York institution Joe Allen located in the Theater District. Joe Allen and Bobby's father were partners, and Allen was so impressed with the young man that he paid for Bobby to attend the world-renowned French Culinary Institute.

Bobby mastered classical cooking techniques and honed his management skills, but he knew that French cuisine was not for him. Instead, Bobby was introduced to foods native to the American Southwest—such as avocados, black and white beans, and chile peppers—after working at several of Jonathan Waxman's restaurants, and he wanted to explore the possibilities of this regional cuisine.

After graduating in 1988, Bobby was hired as the executive chef at a restaurant in New York City's East Village called the Miracle Grill. That's where he started testing ways to wake up standard grilled fare—he's a master of the grill—using bold flavors in particular. It didn't take long for his vivid southwestern dishes to earn him a cult following. Restaurateur Jerome Kretchmer, a regular diner at the Miracle Grill, recognized this kid's potential and offered to back Bobby in a restaurant of his own. It's far more typical for someone to be given a salaried position as executive chef—an offer like Jerome's doesn't come along very often.

Mesa Grill opened up in New York's trendy Flatiron District in 1991, and Bobby, only in his late twenties, became an overnight success. In addition to his success with Mesa Grill, Bobby cultivated a substantial television presence. The first president of the Food Network, Reese Schonfeld, sought Bobby out because of all the press he was getting; he has been part of the network right from the beginning. His first show, called "Grillin' and Chillin,'" featured Bobby as the city boy and Jack McDaniel, a noted chef from the wilds of Philadelphia, as the country boy in overalls and a straw hat.

Bobby became one of the most reliable guests on a show I was producing at the time, called "In Food Today," which was about people, places, and trends in the culinary world. If a guest missed her flight or someone didn't show up, we could count on Bobby to get there in time to do an incredible segment, no matter what the topic. He used to bring his own spices and do great on-the-fly sessions about how to grill something as delicate as shrimp or as basic as chicken. When the taping was over he'd race back to the restaurant without even waiting to collect his saucepans and utensils. He liked the medium and the viewers loved his believable, approachable manner, which is why he probably had more food television shows airing at one time than any other chef. He had another on Lifetime Television for Women called "The Main Ingredient," which was a lifestyle show. In addition, "Hot Off the Grill with Bobby Flay" was running on the Food Network at the same time.

With all of his television responsibilities, you might wonder who was minding the store. Bobby spreads himself thin but the cooking always comes first. "The Main Ingredient" was a daily hour-long show, but he scheduled it so he could be back at Mesa Grill by noon. He doesn't shoot if it's time to change the seasonal menu, and he knows that he has to keep his hands in the pot to make sure the quality is consistent and the hip, funky atmosphere of the restaurant is maintained. Mesa Grill has a large celebrity clientele, which has a lot to do with the cook's outgoing personality, and diners enjoy seeing him there.

One of his specialty dishes at Mesa Grill is spicy tuna tartar wrapped in roasted yellow peppers with crispy tortillas. As an appetizer, he makes blue corn-dusted baby squid, which is served with a green-chile tartar sauce. Another signature dish is blue corn pancakes filled with barbecued duck, topped with a habanero chile sauce. Bobby creates all his own sauces, which include a Mesa hot sauce that's served on crusty hominy cakes accompanied by avocado, pieces of salmon tartare, and a red onion relish. His

roasted poblano sauce comes with pan-fried Chilean sea bass with smoked yellow pepper grits. An oven-roasted lamb shank is served with a serrano vinegar and brown sugar sauce, while another favorite is New Mexican spice-rubbed pork tenderloin with bourbon ancho chile sauce, accompanied by a sweet potato tamale with crushed pecan butter.

Most people tend to think of southwestern food as searingly hot and spicy, but Bobby has mastered cutting the heat with other flavors—perhaps maple syrup or a honey—so that the food delivers a double sensation. You might see similar dishes on other menus, but Bobby's flavor is unexpected and original. Careful attention is also paid to presentation. The tuna tartare arrives nestled on tortilla chips and the colors compliment each other, so multiple senses awaken when the plate is placed in front of you.

In 1993 Bobby opened a second restaurant with Jerome, also in the Flatiron district. Bolo has the same hip atmosphere as Mesa Grill and centers around the wonderful flavors of contemporary Spanish cuisine. Bobby made a smooth transition from southwestern to Latin cooking with dishes like fire-roasted tuna with five-Spanish-spice crust and a black squid ink risotto with grilled prawns and green onion vinaigrette. One of his signature dishes at Bolo is the Pan-Roasted Arctic Char in a Caldo Gallego Broth—caldo gallego is a traditional Spanish white-bean-and-meat based soup with as many variations as minestrone—served with roasted potatoes, Serrano ham, and mussels. That same year, at age twenty-eight, Bobby won a James Beard award for Rising Chef of the Year, and the French Culinary Institute honored him with its first ever Outstanding Graduate Award. The following spring, his first cookbook, *Bold American Food*, was published.

Bobby now has four cookbooks, two television shows, two restaurants, and is also devoted to spending a lot of time with his six-year-old daughter, Sophie. Despite being the master of so many things, Bobby is keenly aware that a chef's reputation is everything. He might spend two days at Bolo, then run back to Mesa, but Bobby's figured out a system by which he can do justice to each of these endeavors.

Good food is a bigger part of people's daily lives than it's ever been before. Many people spend as much time deciding where to eat as they do planning vacations or entertaining. Bobby's restaurants and his personal style embody this trend, in which excellent food is at the heart of the experience but style and atmosphere are essential as well. Bobby's made both Mesa Grill and Bolo into places where people want to go. He's not pretending to be the ultimate authority on a world cuisine. He's a great chef who has put together a dynamic culinary and business plan with a focus on flavor that discriminating diners recognize and appreciate. And even if he spent all his time behind the stove, Bobby would be fine, because his heart is in the kitchen.

Beet and Goat Cheese Empanadas with Orange-Paprika Vinaigrette

Makes 6 appetizer servings

For the vinaigrette
4 cups fresh orange juice
3 tablespoons sherry vinegar
2 teaspoons Dijon mustard
2 teaspoons Spanish paprika
1 tablespoon honey
¾ cup olive oil
   Salt and freshly ground pepper

In a nonreactive saucepan over high heat, reduce the orange juice to ¼ cup. Remove from heat and cool.

Combine the orange syrup, vinegar, mustard, paprika, and honey in a blender and blend for 30 seconds. With the motor running, slowly add the olive oil until the vinaigrette emulsifies.

Season to taste with salt and pepper, then transfer to a squeeze bottle.

For the empanada filling
2 tablespoons olive oil
2 small shallots, thinly sliced
1 large beet, roasted, peeled, and cut into ½-inch dice
4 ounces soft goat cheese
2 scallions, white parts only, finely sliced
2 tablespoons sherry vinegar
Salt and freshly ground pepper

Heat the olive oil in a small sauté pan over medium heat. Add the shallots and cook until soft; remove from heat to let cool slightly. Combine the beets, goat cheese, scallions, sherry vinegar, and shallots, tossing together to mix thoroughly. Season with salt and pepper to taste and set the filling aside.

For the empanadas
4 sheets phyllo dough
¼ pound unsalted butter, melted, plus more for baking sheet

½ bulb fennel, peeled and thinly sliced
¼ pound arugula
   Salt and freshly ground pepper

Preheat the oven to 375°F. Place one sheet of the phyllo dough on a flat work surface and lightly brush with the melted butter. Top with the remaining three sheets phyllo, buttering each one. Cut the stack of phyllo in half lengthwise, then cut each half crosswise into six equal parts. Spoon a heaping tablespoon of the reserved filling onto one end of each strip and form a triangle by folding the upper right-hand corner to the opposite side, as you would fold a flag. Continue folding until all the strips are used. (You will have twelve empanadas.)

Place the triangles on a buttered baking sheet, brush the tops with the remaining melted butter, and bake until golden brown, 8 to 10 minutes.

Toss the fennel and arugula with the vinaigrette to taste and season with salt and pepper. Divide the salad among six salad plates, top with the empanadas, and serve.

Bernard Carmouche

Food saved Bernard Carmouche from an uncertain future. He was born in 1967, in a rough part of New Orleans called Uptown. His dad, who drove tourists around in a cab, and his mother, a hospital aide, raised their two sons and six daughters to aspire to a safe city job with a good pension. His high school had a co-op program, so Bernard took two buses across town every afternoon to wash dishes at the Bonanza Steak House for four dollars and fifty cents an hour. The steak house had an all-you-can-eat salad bar, and Bernard still shudders at the memory of scrubbing those rough wooden salad bowls night after night. Half of his paycheck went to his parents to help out with household expenses, one quarter went into the bank, and the rest was spending money.

An older man in the neighborhood was a crew chief, in charge of hiring the dishwashers and janitors for the famous Cajun and Creole restaurant Commander's Palace. He told Bernard and a few other kids that he had a couple of full-time openings for dish-washers. Bernard's buddies thought they were too cool for the job, and it meant working until 2 A.M., but it was only a trolley ride from his home and Bernard said yes.

One day there was a lot of buzz in the kitchen about a new chef coming in from Providence, Rhode Island, a French-Canadian without much experience with New Orleans food. Less than a year later, Emeril Lagasse was making a name for himself at Commander's Palace. One evening, a few months into his new job, Bernard was glumly confronting a huge stack of pots when one of the garde-manger—a New Orleans term for the person who supervises the salad making—asked Bernard for some help cutting strawberries. Seeing the teenager's face light up, Emeril came over and asked him if he'd like to learn how to cook.

Emeril made it clear that the cooking lessons were contingent on Bernard finishing high school. He made Bernard show him his report card every quarter, giving him twenty dollars for every "A" and ten dollars for every "B." To motivate him further, Emeril placed him in charge of the pantry and hot appetizers, gradually leading him up the ranks from prep cook, to the hot line, the back line, first cook, and eventually to sous-chef. After graduation, Bernard began to understand that food could be his way out of

poverty. Although he wanted to take out a student loan to attend culinary school, Emeril dissuaded him. He said, "I will teach you everything I know, I'll let you stand side by side with me, but you're going to have to put in the hours and do what it takes."

For two years they would meet at Commander's Palace, sometimes as early as 5 A.M. when Emeril was getting the day's menus together and starting sauces. Some mornings Bernard would come in alone, with butterflies in his stomach, perhaps to start the roue. Sometimes Emeril made comments, and sometimes he made the boy start over from scratch—it was Bernard's apprenticeship. There were forty cooks in the kitchen, but Bernard was the one Emeril really nourished.

Eight years after he arrived in New Orleans, Emeril announced that he'd gotten the backing to start a place of his own. He offered to take his protégé with him, but Bernard had both experience and stability at Commander's Palace and figured he should stick with it. Also taking note of Bernard's talent, Ellen Brennan, whose family owns Commander's Palace, sent him to train to be a sous-chef at their restaurant in Houston. When he returned to New Orleans in 1992, he opened up a new place in the French Quarter for the Brennans. Called the Palace Café, it offered the same classic New Orleans dishes in a more casual setting.

Bernard was in his eighth month there as executive sous-chef when Emeril invited him to dinner. Emeril talked about how he

and all chefs have a headache with constant kitchen staff turnover. They invest a great deal in training people, many of whom leave when their heart isn't in it. After listening to his mentor's war stories, Bernard went back to the Brennans and resigned. Emeril had offered him the title of sous-chef at his namesake restaurant, but Bernard's answer was, "No I want to be a cook, to learn how to make the contemporary Creole dishes you offer, and we'll take it from there." Bernard quickly became his mentor's right-hand man, the person Emeril trusted to speak for him if he was away from the restaurant.

In 1995, Bernard seized the opportunity to intern with Roger Vergé in the South of France. Soon after that, encouraged by the success of "Emeril Live!" Universal Studios approached Emeril to open up a restaurant at City Walk, a group of stores and restaurants just outside the studio entrance in Orlando, Florida. Realizing he couldn't be everywhere at once, Emeril asked Bernard if he would take charge of the new restaurant as executive chef. Fine dining had never been attempted in this locale, so it was a somewhat risky proposition. It also meant relocating his wife—Bernard had married his high school sweetheart—and two kids to Florida. And it meant stepping out from behind Emeril and really being tested.

Bernard rolled up his sleeves and took on the task, from overseeing the construction of the building to hiring almost two hundred employees, locating purveyors, and organizing the kitchen. Nothing happened at Emeril's Orlando without Bernard's approval. Assuming these responsibilities under Emeril's name was enormously stressful, but the Orlando Sentinel soon recognized Bernard's contributions in an article titled, "Passion Flavors His Creations."

Bernard draws on his vibrant Cajun and Creole culinary heritage for his inventive daily degustation menus. He owes his success as a chef in his own right to the superb training he received from culinary masters, but also to the cooking he loved in his grandmother's kitchen. The menu emphasizes seafood, with appetizers like pecan-crusted queen snapper with crispy sweet potato gaufrettes and haricots vert, and cumin-seared ahi tuna, served with a jicama, cucumber, and red onion relish. Entrees include pan crispy red snapper served with saffron rice pilaf, fava beans, crawfish tails, cipollini onions, and baby fennel; a pesto roasted white sea bass with purple Peruvian potatoes; lump crab meat, wax bean relish, and a tomato balsamic butter sauce. For the meat-lover, there's a venison tenderloin served with a lobster potato cake and shaved portobello mushrooms.

Now that he does the hiring, Bernard often chooses people without any food background, as long as they have a passion for cooking. He believes they make the best students, and says, "Since someone believed in me, it's my duty to give others the same chance." Bernard turned an opportunity into a winning hand in life. As humble as they come, he is now mentoring a whole new generation of aspiring chefs, and they are truly lucky.

Sautéed Rainbow Trout

Makes 4 servings

4 rainbow trout fillets (6 ounces each), skin on
  Salt and pepper
  Juice of 1 lemon plus lemon slices, for garnish
1 tablespoon olive oil
  Fresh parsley, for garnish

Preheat the oven to 475°F.

Season the fillets on both sides with salt and pepper and a squeeze of lemon. Place a large sauté pan over medium-high heat and add the olive oil. Add the fillets, skin-sides down, to the hot pan and cook for 3 minutes. Transfer the fish to the broiler and cook for 2 more minutes.

Divide the fish among four serving plates. Garnish with the lemon slices and parsley and serve immediately.

Allan Vernon

I've never been to Jamaica, but a friend of mine who is part Jamaican used to endlessly sing the praises of Vernon's Jerk Paradise. One day we were in the mood for Caribbean food and headed over to the restaurant on West 29th Street in New York City. I remember thinking how transporting the atmosphere was. Palm trees were painted on shockingly green walls; reggae music was playing; the waiters had dreadlocks stuffed under bright yellow and red knit caps; and after a couple of glasses of rum punch, I felt like I was in Montego Bay.

When I looked at the menu, I felt as though it was a "Jeopardy" cooking category, because everything was jerk: jerk chicken, jerk lamb, jerk beef, even jerk salmon and jerk scallops. Of course each dish came with fried plantains, rice, and beans, and the menu did offer a few other things, like curried chicken and curried goat, beef patties, goat's head soup, and cow cod soup (the broth is made from the cow's testicles, and fish is added at the end). My friend tried to get me to sample some of the more exotic dishes she'd grown up on, but since I wanted to play it safe on that first visit, I decided on the jerk chicken.

After we'd ordered, a very tall, dark-skinned man with a beautiful smile and a voice so deep it immediately got your attention walked into the room. That was the chef and owner, Allan Vernon, but I didn't realize it at the time. Vernon—his friends call him by his last name—was working the tables, charming the women, telling people how no one made jerk chicken like he did, and brandishing a bottle of sauce. I burst out laughing, and he turned to me and said, "What's so funny?"

"I've never seen anyone so proud of his cooking and his sauce," I replied. I've never been so embarrassed in my life as when I saw his picture on the label of the sauce, and it clicked: this is Allan Vernon. I wanted to sink under the table.

He said, "Girl, you must have never had jerk before." I shook my head—he had me. He pulled up a chair (he had no idea I worked for the Food Network), introduced himself, and asked how old I was. When I told him I was twenty-three, he said, "You're laughing at me, and you've never had jerk?"

Vernon takes jerk very seriously. Growing up right outside of Kingston, in Mandeville, Jamaica, his family would cook every night in back of the house on a grill fashioned from rocks and scrap metal. Vernon's mother would make a big batch of jerk that would last for a while. She made him help, by cleaning the chicken, picking the peppers for the sauce, going to the store, and washing the dishes. He was her chopper and sous-chef, and she taught him the nitty-gritty of running a kitchen—quite against his wishes!

Jerk brings a dish to life. In Jamaica jerk is both a verb and a noun, and it's available as a fast food in roadside shacks all over the island. Jerk is a process of spicing, marinating, and grilling foods. The three main ingredients are chile pepper (typically a Scotch bonnet pepper, a variety of the habanero pepper and arguably the hottest in the world), allspice berry (not the ground spice combination in pumpkin pies, but the berry of the evergreen pimento, a native West Indian tree), and thyme. Other ingredients, depending on the recipe, include garlic, onion, soy sauce, vinegar, cinnamon, cloves, and ginger. A main ingredient like chicken or pork might be slowly smoked for several days, which softens the meat so it melts in your mouth. The longer it's marinated, the more flavorful the dish becomes. Vernon told me that the cooking process was introduced to Jamaica by the Maroons, African slaves who escaped from the British during the invasion of 1655. They combined the slow cooking method with seasonings used by the local Arawak Indians to preserve meat in a hot climate. Jerk is spicy enough to heat up your mouth and satisfy people who like really spicy food, but not to the point of discomfort. And it's habit-forming.

Vernon missed his mother's jerk when he moved to England to become a telephone technician after graduating from high school. After that he moved to the United States to become a construction worker and, while he enjoyed both jobs, cooking was always his hobby. At get-togethers with family and friends in Queens he was always the one at the grill, cooking foods from Jamaica, jerk in particular. He dreamed of opening up an authentic Jamaican restaurant in New York City, but without any collateral that meant saving up over the years, putting together a business plan, and eventually getting a loan that enabled him, in 1982, to open Vernon's New Jerk House in the northeast Bronx. Perhaps the country's first restaurant to serve jerk specialties, Vernon's attracted diners from all over the city to sample his Jamaican barbecue and meet the charismatic "King of Jerk."

In 1990 he opened Vernon's Jerk Paradise, a funky, out-there Jamaican joint in Manhattan's Garment District. His jerk was so delicious that diners would ask him where they could buy it. Vernon had so much confidence in his sauce that he heeded his customers' advice and decided to bottle it. Without the slightest idea of how enormously difficult it is to place a product in stores, without a publicist or any food marketers, he found a factory that could replicate his exact recipe. He sent a bottle with a letter stating, "Please try my product and let me know what you think," to Molly O'Neill, who wrote a weekly column in the *New York Times* about new food products. To say O'Neill fell in love with the recipe is an understatement—the very next week there was a long story about Vernon and his sauce in the *Times*, in which she christened him the "King of Jerk." Molly O'Neill put Vernon on the map, and after that the phone began to ring off the hook. Right after the review he walked into Zabar's, a premier gourmet food store on Manhattan's Upper West Side, and handed his sauce to owner Murray Klein. Two weeks later, Vernon had shelf space in

Zabar's. From convenience stores to all the gourmet websites, Vernon's sauce is now known worldwide. And people stood in line to eat at Vernon's Jerk Paradise.

Unfortunately the restaurant closed in 1998 after Vernon lost his lease to a developer who wanted the space for a showroom. Because Vernon had painted those green walls himself and poured his heart into the restaurant, it was a sad occasion, but the continued success of his sauce kept his spirits up. Even though the city now boasts several enclaves of Jamaican restaurants and island groceries, you can still get an eight-dollar plateful of the best jerk in the city at Vernon's New Jerk House in Eastchester, in the Bronx. He's thinking up a game plan at that barbecue, while grilling the jerk that's been a staple for him and his community through the lean times and the flush ones—I bet his friends back in Jamaica can even smell it. Wherever Vernon next sets up shop, people will find him, because he is the king.

Vernon's Jerk Baby Back Ribs

Makes 6 to 8 servings

2 slabs baby back ribs (4 to 5 pounds)

For the jerk seasoning
2 Scotch bonnet chile peppers, finely chopped
5 sprigs fresh thyme
6 scallions, both white and green parts, chopped
3 garlic cloves, finely chopped
¼ cup ground allspice
Salt and freshly ground pepper

For the jerk sauce
1 cup Vernon's Jerk Sauce
1 cup water
½ cup red wine

Place the seasoning ingredients in a pot large enough to hold all the ribs. Add water until the pot is three-fourths full. Bring the water to a boil, add the ribs, and boil them for 1 hour. Remove the ribs from the pot and arrange them in a nonreactive baking pan so that they don't overlap.

Preheat the oven to 400°F. Mix the sauce ingredients together and pour the sauce over the ribs. Bake for 30 minutes.

Serve the ribs warm with additional jerk sauce, if desired.

Michael Lomonaco

The late Patrick Clark was executive chef at New York City's Tavern on the Green located in Central Park. He'd wrap up the kitchen around midnight , and occasionally I'd stop by and we'd ride the train home to New Jersey together. One night he was complaining about how hard it is to find good cooks who understand a chef's formula and stay with the restaurant. "The one story that I always tell aspiring chefs is about a driver for a car service I met one night in New York City," he reminisced. When he got into the car that night in 1982, the young driver gave him a second look and asked, "Are you Patrick Clark?"

Identifying himself as an aspiring actor, the driver told Patrick that he'd appeared in Woody Allen's *Broadway Danny Rose* and a few other feature films, but admitted that he was thinking of changing careers. Cooking professionally was one of the ideas he found appealing, and over the course of that ride he grilled Patrick about where he had trained and how long it had taken him to rise through the ranks. Patrick had learned the basics of becoming a chef and running a restaurant by attending New York City Technical College's two-year hotel and restaurant management course. "Taking that course will make you or break you," he told the kid. "It's the best advice I could give you—along with choosing something that you like to do, so you enjoy going to work in the morning."

The driver, of course, was Michael Lomonaco, and to this day he says that ride changed his life. What touched him the most was Patrick's evident delight in being a chef and his combination of energy and inner peace. It was a forty-five-minute drive to Patrick's home in Hillsboro, New Jersey, but Michael almost felt guilty for collecting the fare. He sat on the chef's advice for six months or so, but when his big acting break failed to materialize, he enrolled at New York City Technical College. Michael graduated in 1984, grateful that cooking American food was becoming a legitimate alternative to French cooking or specializing in a single cuisine. In 1986 he was lucky to land an excellent position as a line cook at Le Cirque, under executive chef Alain Sailhac, the French chef who also trained Daniel Boulud, Le Cirque's sous-chef at the time.

Michael's next break came eighteen months later, when he was appointed sous-chef at the 21 Club in Midtown Manhattan, later becoming the executive chef. The 21 Club is known more as an exclusive men's club than for its cuisine. Because the regulars liked standard meat-and-potatoes fare at their power lunches, Michael had to work with the menu that they were accustomed to. But after the restaurant got three stars from *New York Newsday*, a broader clientele started coming in at night for dishes like pepper-boosted crab cakes, rack of lamb with lemon-scented

orzo, pan-roasted quail with couscous, and his celebrated roasted Maine lobster potpie with tarragon biscuits. Michael's cooking is regional American, with an emphasis on the best local products available on a seasonal basis. He cooks a lot with game: squab, venison, and wild buck antelope from Texas. The James Beard Award team looks for people whose food justifies the buzz, and in 1989 he was named one of New York City's great chefs.

In 1996, Michael started his own show on the Food Network called "Michael's Place." He'd had experience with lighting and props, so he came to the table with an understanding of television production. Viewers were meant to feel they were at Michael's apartment, and he cooked American comfort food. You could learn anything from how to make mashed potatoes or cook a roast perfectly to arranging a less familiar ingredient like couscous around a staple like baked chicken. He also hosted a show on the Discovery Channel called "Epicurious," in which he traveled the world in search of food stories. This was a real departure from typical cooking shows and also made the most of his acting talent. Typically a chef's personality dictates the confines of the show, but a talent like Michael's can be paired with just about any subject. So in the end Michael ended up not having to choose between acting and cooking—and he's a showman in the kitchen too.

In 1997 Michael moved to the Windows on the World restaurant on the one hundred and seventh floor of One World Trade Tower. At the time, it had a celebrated wine cellar and a solid reputation as a place tourists went for the view and a decent meal, but the food wasn't the high point. Michael always felt that with its view of the Statue of Liberty and the Empire State Building, Windows on the World had a uniquely American spirit that should be reflected in the cuisine as well. He translated that feeling into

dishes, rounding up ingredients from all over the United States, from Maine lobster and Plymouth flounder fresh off the boat to organic produce from California.

At the 21 Club he'd been doing about two hundred covers a day, and now he was responsible for eight hundred. Michael wasn't afraid of running a bigger space, because he's an excellent manager. He's able to hire people at the top tier who will be faithful to his way of doing things, and he treats his workers like family. He allows his employees to go home if they suffer a headache, or they can leave early to pick up their kids. Michael is compassionate and not afraid to show it, and he's deeply loyal in his personal relationships as well. When Patrick Clark passed away in 1998, both Michael and I took it very hard. I asked his widow if I could say something at the funeral, to remind people of Patrick's talent and his important contributions to the culinary world, but I was afraid I wasn't going to be able to make it through without breaking down. Michael coached me and planted himself right in my field of vision, so that when I came close to tears I'd meet his eyes and feel his support.

Over the next few years, Windows on the World joined the list of New York's finest restaurants, becoming less of a tourist spot and more of a destination for foodies. As the chef and director of all culinary operations, Michael oversaw the menus, the hiring, and the food ordering for the main dining room, Wild Blue, a more intimate restaurant in the same space, and the Greatest Bar on Earth, which served bar food. He was in charge and made the place his own, refusing to be categorized. Just as his energy and multiethnic touches enlivened the traditional menu at the 21 Club, Michael reinterpreted American classics for appreciative diners at Windows on the World.

These restaurants also made breakfast for their business clientele, so Michael got to work early. Usually he showed his security card and headed up to the one hundred and seventh floor. But he'd been needing new reading glasses for a couple of weeks, and on September eleventh, he stopped in at the Lenscrafters on the shopping concourse level of the World Trade Center. He was being fitted for glasses when the building was evacuated by shouts of, "Get out of the building, get out of the building!" Michael ran a block or two, turned to look back, and realized that the plane had hit the tower just below Windows on the World. Immediately he thought of the cooks, the hostesses, the accounting people, and the manager, Christine Olender there planning a new wine cellar with the builders who also perished.

So many people whom Michael worked with died that day. He went from being a chef to helping the FBI figure out who was missing and contacting their grieving families, some of whom were left with nothing. He also helped found a foundation called Windows of Hope, and planned a fundraiser on October eleventh where restaurants all around the world donated a percentage of that night's proceeds. The money went to the families of all the missing food professionals who worked in all the restaurants and food service jobs in the World Trade Center. He continues to make this one of his top priorities and he is committed to bringing the people he used to work with together again. Of course Michael has been sought out since the tragedy, and he's working with the owner of the former Windows on the World to find a new home in Manhattan for his contemporary American cuisine. Michael is hard at work on a book project and is planning his own restaurant, Lomonaco's, in Manhattan right now. I have no doubt that he will succeed, because he has the talent and the will, and most importantly has not forgotten where he came from.

Pan-Roasted Foie Gras with White Peach–Chile Relish

Makes 4 to 6 appetizer servings

For the relish
- ¼ cup white vinegar
- ¼ cup loosely packed light brown sugar
- 2 tablespoons finely chopped shallots
- ¼ cup finely chopped red jalapeño peppers
- 2 tablespoons raisins
- 1 tablespoon finely chopped garlic
- 1 tablespoon grated fresh ginger
- ½ teaspoon salt
- 6 firm, fresh white peaches (about 1½ pounds), blanched to remove the skin, pitted, and sliced

For the foie gras and croutons
- 1 pound fresh duck foie gras (see Note)
  Salt and pepper
- 12 slices baguette, brushed with olive oil and toasted in a hot oven

Bring the vinegar and sugar to a boil in a medium saucepan. Add the shallots, jalapeños, raisins, garlic, ginger, and salt and simmer, uncovered, for 5 minutes. Add the peaches and simmer an additional 5 minutes before removing from heat. Cool for 15 minutes, then serve or transfer to an airtight container and refrigerate for up to 1 week.

Clean the foie gras, using a small paring knife to remove any veins, bile, or other imperfections. Cut into ½-inch-thick slices, approximately 2 to 3 ounces each. Season the slices with salt and pepper to taste just before cooking. Heat a dry, heavy-bottomed sauté pan until very hot. Place the foie gras slices in the pan and sear quickly on both sides. Serve on a bed of warm peach relish with the sliced baguette croutons.

Note: The raw, fresh duck or goose liver known as foie gras comes from specially raised fowl that produce a liver much larger and fattier than an ordinary duck or goose liver. Foie gras is generally sold as grades A, B, or C. Grade A is the best quality and most expensive; it's usually free of most blemishes and requires the least time to clean.

Mario Batali

Producers rarely book guests without meeting them in advance. But "In Food Today" was a daily live show, and in a pinch you do what is necessary to get a guest—and it had better be a good one! One day during our 1994 season Mario Batali's name came up when we needed to find a replacement guest. So I called his restaurant at the time, Po, in New York City's West Village. It was around noon, so he must have been prepping for dinner when he answered the phone. I introduced myself and got straight to the point: "Look, a guest cancelled today. The theme of the segment is Italian food, and I'm calling to see if you might be available." When he asked me what he would have to do I explained, "This is a national show, you'll have to cook and demonstrate a dish and be interviewed by both hosts. And it's live." He was clearly willing to give it a shot, but I needed to make sure he knew what he was getting into. "How many times have you been on television?" I pressed. "We don't even have time to shop for the ingredients for you." Mario started laughing, and said simply, "I'm Italian, I can do this." Delighted, I hung up the phone, and was preparing the pre-interview—a brief write-up about the guest so that the host knows what to expect—when I realized I'd forgotten something. Getting Mario on the phone again, I confessed that I had neglected to go over the dish he was planning to cook. "Something classic, a spaghetti bolognese," he replied.

When my production assistant came in that afternoon to tell me Mario Batali had arrived, I could tell by her expression that something had thrown her for a loop. When I first saw him in the green room, I know my jaw dropped. In contrast to the standard clean-cut short-haired look of most chefs, Mario has a long red ponytail. He had on a chef's jacket and the classic long kitchen apron, but it looked as though white socks and orange clogs were all that he was wearing underneath it. (I had him leave the room ahead of me, and was relieved to see that he was in fact in cut-off jeans.) "Do you always dress like this?" I asked. "Every night," he replied. Winter, too, it turns out.

Mario is a one-man trendsetter. Just as he doesn't care what people think about the way he dresses, he doesn't mind diverging from traditional recipes. Chefs tend to be categorized according to whether they cook classic Italian food or focus on Italian-American cuisine but Mario pays little attention. He can prepare standard Italian dishes like the bolognese sauce he made that day for hosts Donna Hanover and David Rosengarten, but he's not afraid to enhance recipes by adding butter, egg, and white truffles to pappardelle or making linguine with pancetta and clams. Mario's cooking revolves around the fresh, simple ingredients that cooks in Italy rely on: aromatic herbs, great vegetables, wonderful cheeses. He makes ravioli with calves' brains and gnocchi with oxtails. He offers a pasta tasting menu that builds on the framework of the pasta to introduce pure, unorthodox flavors in dishes like three-cheese ravioli and goose liver ravioli with balsamic vinegar and brown butter.

Mario moved to Spain from Seattle with his family when he was fourteen and attended high school in Madrid. His plan was to get his university degree in the United States and return to Spain and become a banker. But after obtaining a bachelor's degree with a double major in finance and Spanish theater from Rutgers University, Mario found that the suit-and-tie world of finance wasn't for him. His father still makes his own pasta and sausage and wine in Seattle, and food very much held the family together. Almost on a whim, Mario applied to the Cordon Bleu Academy of Culinary Arts in London, but quickly dropped out because he simply didn't find it intense enough. An apprenticeship with the legendary London chef Marco White proved more educational, and Mario cooked all over France. In 1984 he returned to the States and began cooking on the West Coast, first for a large catering hall, then as a chef at the Four Seasons Hotel in San Francisco, then at the legendary Biltmore Hotel in Santa Barbara. The hotel chain asked Mario to move to Hawaii, but instead he moved back to Italy. He spent three years in the tiny northern Italian town of Borgo Caponne, cooking in a small restaurant that was situated on the main road that ran through town. The restaurant had its own garden where Mario picked the peppers and lettuce and tomatoes for the day's meals, an experience that taught him how to appreciate the freshest local ingredients and informed his ideas about simple Italian cooking.

In 1992 he moved to New York City, this time to Greenwich Village, to help a family friend re-vamp his classic Italian restaurant, Rocco. Mario opened Po in 1993. Seating only thirty-four people, Po is aptly named, since po is slang for "small" in Italian. Devoted patrons, word of mouth, and a terrific *New York Times* review put Po on the map and gave it a reputation as the place to go for simple, exquisite Italian food. The timing was also good for his foray into television, because the Food Network was born that same year. Mario was young, he had a hip look, and his Italian food was simple enough for viewers to make at home. After appearing on a few shows as a guest, Mario got his own show, "Molto Mario." His repertoire has expanded from Italy to the Mediterranean basin in his second show, "Mediterranean Mario," in which he travels to the regions where dishes have originated and shows how local climate and geography affect flavors and ingredients.

Mario was also lucky in love, meeting Susi Cahn through the business in 1994. Susi's father Miles owns Coach Farm, which makes superb goat cheese in Pine Plains, New York. In the summer she grows some of Mario's specialty vegetables on the farm, including greens and herbs, heirloom tomatoes, different kinds of beets, beans, and squashes. Mario's marriage clearly nurtures him. Chefs with his profile need more than an entourage. They need one person in their corner, no matter what, and Susi's right there, all the time.

In 1998, Mario and Joe Bastianich, Lidia's son, got together, renovated the old Carriage House in the Village, and opened Babbo. The move raised some eyebrows because they're competitors, but Mario and Joe wanted a place that served a more modern Italian cuisine. As executive chef, Mario welcomed the chance to expand from the physical and culinary confines of Po. Opening up the new place involved a lot of headaches and many months of fifteen-hour days, but it paid off. In 1998 Babbo won the James Beard Award for Best New Restaurant in New York, and the *New York Times* gave it three stars. Babbo specializes in regional Italian dishes with Mario-only touches, like goat cheese tortellini dusted in dried orange and wild fennel pollen, or a spicy lamb sausage served with "mint love letters"—rectangular ravioli filled with a mint and a sweet pea pesto.

A year later Mario sold Po and went on to open a Roman-style trattoria called Lupa, also in Greenwich Village. Less formal than Babbo, Lupa has a rowdy front room for walk-ins and a more intimate, reservations-only rear dining room. Lupa serves trattoria fare, with the innovative Batali touch apparent in dishes like tuna belly with raisins and cumin, sweet-marinated grilled quail, and a thick fillet of fried baccala (salt cod), served on a bed of fennel strips. He and Joe also own a place called Esca, in Manhattan's Theater District, which focuses on the freshest seafood imaginable, with an emphasis on crudo: fish and shellfish served raw, brushed with olive oil and complimented by surprising flavors like anise and salsa verde. Whole sea bass roasted in a sea salt crust cracked open at the table is a house specialty. The common denominator is Italy, but Mario doesn't choose between the Old and the New

Worlds, and his menus and venues give diners the choice as well. In another venture with Joe Bastianich, Mario opened up a wine shop in Union Square called Italian Wine Merchants. All the bottles on the shelves are for display only. After you make your selection, the staff retrieves it from the cellar, where all the wine is stored at the correct temperature. Mario samples each wine before offering it his restaurants, and he wanted to make his wine list available to consumers. It's another way to spread the word about an important aspect of Italian cuisine.

Mario is a man with a lot on his plate, but fortunately, he's great at juggling. He focuses on one priority at a time, whether it's buying a stove, or choosing where to buy broccoli rabe. He's always looking for the right vehicles to make it happen, and his energy and instincts are the right combination to make him a success.

Neapolitan Ravioli
Ravioli alla Napolitana

Makes 4 servings

For the pasta
3½ cups flour, plus more for work surface
 4 large eggs
 1 tablespoon olive oil

For the filling
 3 cups whole-milk ricotta cheese
1½ cups freshly grated pecorino cheese
 1 bunch fresh parsley, chopped (about ¼ cup)
 2 large eggs
 1 bunch fresh basil, leaves only, cut into chiffonade (about ¼ cup)
¼ pound prosciutto, cut into ⅛-inch dice
   Several gratings of fresh nutmeg
 8 tablespoons unsalted butter

To make the pasta dough: Place the flour in a mound in the center of a large wooden cutting board. Make a well in the middle and add the eggs and olive oil. Using a fork, beat together the eggs and oil and begin to incorporate the flour, starting with the inner rim of the well. As you expand the well, keep pushing the flour up from the bottom to retain the well shape. (Do not worry that this initial phase looks messy. The dough will start to come together when half of the flour is incorporated.)

Push the pieces of dough and any unincorporated flour together and start kneading the dough, using the palms of both hands. Once the dough has formed a cohesive mass, remove it from the board. Scrape up any leftover crusty bits and discard them. Lightly flour the board and continue kneading for 3 more minutes; the dough should be elastic and a little sticky. Continue to knead for another 3 minutes, dusting your board with more flour when necessary. Form a smooth ball of dough, wrap it in plastic, and allow it to rest for 30 minutes at room temperature.

To make the filling: Meanwhile, put the ricotta and pecorino in a large bowl and mix well. Add the parsley, eggs, basil, prosciutto, and nutmeg and stir thoroughly to combine. Set aside.

To shape the ravioli: Start by rolling out the dough to less than ¹⁄₁₆ inch thick—that's the lowest setting on a roller-type pasta machine. Place the sheet of pasta on a lightly floured work surface.

If you have a ravioli-cutting rolling pin, cover one half of the sheet of pasta with a ¼-inch-thick layer of the ricotta mixture. Fold the other half of the pasta over and press down lightly with your hands. Carefully roll the two sheets together with the roller to form the ravioli. Using a scalloped pastry cutter, cut the ravioli apart along the score lines formed by the rolling pin.

If you do not have a ravioli-cutting rolling pin, then use a scalloped pastry cutter to cut the single sheet of pasta into 2- by 1-inch rectangles. Place a teaspoon of the ricotta mixture in the center of a rectangle and fold the pasta over it, like a piece of notebook paper, then pinch the edges to form a one-inch square. Repeat until all the pasta and ricotta mixture have been used.

To cook the ravioli: Bring 8 quarts water to a boil, and add 3 tablespoons of salt. Drop the ravioli in and cook 6 to 7 minutes, until tender and cooked through. Meanwhile, in a large sauté pan, heat the butter over medium heat until melted and bubbling. Emulsify it with 4 tablespoons pasta water from the pasta pot. Thoroughly drain the ravioli, add it to the sauté pan, and toss with the butter for 1 minute to coat. Serve immediately.

Jimmy Bannos

Any visitor going to Chicago knows about the Sears Tower and Wrigley Field. However few realize some of the best Cajun cuisine in the country is in the Windy City. In May of 1999 my executive producer, Karen Katz, and I were there working on an outdoor cooking show, which we wanted to be a sort of culinary concert and a week's worth of "Emeril Live in Chicago!" shows. We were looking for characters who could tell the kind of story about food that makes you want to listen, whether it's the food or the chef that does the talking. People who knew we worked with Emeril Lagasse automatically suggested Cajun and Creole, even though we wanted to try something different. But they insisted that a place called Heaven on Seven, located in downtown Chicago's "Loop," had the best Cajun food north of the bayou, so we decided to check it out.

My taste buds were thinking crawfish and andouille with red beans and rice, and I wasn't expecting to walk into an office building. But as soon as we walked into Heaven on Seven, we were transported to a bayou roadhouse, a warm space with a laid-back atmosphere. Zydeco music was playing, people were relaxing with their elbows on the table, and the walls were covered with Mardi Gras memorabilia and pictures of the bayou.

Huge menu boards on the walls popped out at us, describing the specials of the day: gumbo, crayfish, jambalaya. As we waited at the bar for our table, we ran into Tommy Corneal, from George Corneal and Sons, one of Chicago's biggest fresh fruit and vegetable purveyors whom we had met earlier in the day. He said, "You guys came to a great place. I want to introduce you to my main man Jimmy." I'd never encountered such a relaxed way to present a chef, a manner that emphasized his accessibility rather than his importance, and I really liked it. And when the chef came out of the kitchen, Tommy remarked, "Hey, Jimmy, meet my new friends from Food Network."

Jimmy appeared in chef's whites, wearing his signature red bandanna wrapped around his forehead to catch the sweat. He radiates energy, and talks about his Creole creations the way a dad might brag about his son's home runs. He said, "Are you ready to go to the bayou? Because I'm going to take you there." As we had a drink he recommended his favorites: hot bayou cakes made of crawfish, shrimp and crab meat with a spicy rémoulade sauce, and angry mussels smothered in garlic—a dish that is served steaming hot and heats up the palate as well. He started us off with a tomato stack: slices of tomato piled up, drizzled with olive oil, and sprinkled with herb-crusted goat cheese. It wasn't a typical Cajun dish, but it had its own intensity and spice, which I found unusual. And as the meal went on, I realized that Jimmy served a lot of standard Creole dishes but also had his own way of specializing them.

Jimmy makes dishes that take some imagination to pull off, and they taste great. For example, I'd never heard of such a thing as steak gumbo. It still has a roue, but he replaces the chicken and seafood with an Angus ribeye and garlic mashed potatoes. Shrimp and andouille egg rolls are another inspired concoction. Only Jimmy could master dishes like this because they represent his unique interpretation of Cajun. He's not pretending to own that cuisine—instead he innovatively uses Cajun ingredients and

techniques. But Jimmy is no stranger to traditional southern favorites. He served me collard greens that were better than the ones I've tried at many celebrated soul food restaurants.

On the way to our table, we passed the "Wall of Flame," which contains over two thousand different hot sauces. The wild labels and the vibrant greens and oranges and blood reds made it seem as though all that heat was taking on a life of its own. Like Jimmy himself, the wall has a big presence and attracts a following. In addition to the wall, there are twenty-six varieties of hot sauce right on the table, and I can only imagine how spicy some of them are, particularly the one labeled "Hot as a Mutha."

You don't have to look far to find where the food is prepared at Heaven on Seven, because Jimmy is a showman and created an large open kitchen. Every cook and dishwasher is part of the performance, and it's fun to watch the cooks in action since they are completely absorbed in making what you're about to eat. The restaurant is equipped with an old diner counter with a row of seats that look directly into the kitchen. Although Heaven on Seven is far from fancy, there's a six-week waiting list for those seats. Instead of having wine with your meal, you sip a Hurricane—a New Orleans cocktail made with rum, fruit juice, and grenadine. It's like getting a first-class ticket to New Orleans without having to get on a plane.

Jimmy's wildly original dishes like crawfish and spinach in phyllo, muffaletta calzone, and orzolaya (jambalaya made with orzo pasta) reflect his Greek background. He grew up in an Italian neighborhood in Chicago, bussing tables and greeting guests in his parents' classic Greek coffee shop. In 1980 he and his brother and parents opened up the New Garland Coffee Shop on the seventh floor of the Garland Building. Always fascinated by New Orleans food and culture, Jimmy and his wife Annamarie headed south after cooking school to immerse themselves in the regional flavors of the bayou. Between stints at the family coffee shop, he cooked with legends like Paul Prudhomme, Emeril Lagasse, and Frank Brigsten. Customers in Chicago began demanding more of Jimmy's Cajun dishes because there was no

other place in town to get that kind of food. In between blue-plate specials and Reuben sandwiches he was serving up pints of gumbo.

In 1985, the family took a leap and transformed the coffee shop into Heaven on Seven. Jimmy's understandably proud of having made this successful transition. The name came to him in the shower, as he was getting ready for a press interview about the new restaurant. Jimmy said to himself, "We're on the seventh floor and my food will make people feel as though they're in heaven." The rest is Chicago culinary history.

It's not unusual for a chef with Jimmy's energy to check on a table half way through the meal, but when Jimmy showed up at ours he was actually carrying bowls of soup and sat down at the table. "I had to bring this over myself, because it's my specialty, turtle soup," he announced. I almost fainted. How could I eat a turtle? But when a chef brings a dish to the table, there's no turning back. Jimmy went on about the virtues of turtle meat, also explaining that it's served at formal Mardi Gras balls and considered a great delicacy. It was Louisiana turtle with smoked Tasso (Cajun ham) and pickled pork. I'd never tasted anything like it, and I must admit it was really good—rich and intensely flavored.

Many chefs obsess about what people are saying about their food, the quality of their service, and who dines at their restaurants, but not Jimmy. People tell him that in order to become a star he should be doing French or perhaps Italian cuisine. But he's a down-home Chicago boy with a passion for making New Orleans cuisine his own. Jimmy joined us on one of the shows we taped in Chicago to talk about his impact on the city's culinary scene, and his energy and charisma won the audience over instantly.

Jimmy has claimed his territory in Chicago, and he's here to stay, noting, "There's too much pizza and plenty of Asian, but this is the only place you can get real Cajun." Now there are three restaurants and a cookbook called *Heaven on Seven* for fans outside the Chicago area—but there's nothing quite like a visit to the original restaurant. The place has history and you can feel it. Jimmy walks around the dining room, checking on the food and the service, joking with patrons, relaxed and in his element. He makes it feel like a party, and that's his charm.

Chicken-and-Shrimp Orzoffee

Makes 6 servings

For the orzoffee

    5 ounces dried orzo
    1 pound boneless, skinless chicken breasts, cut into ½-inch pieces
    1 tablespoon plus ¼ teaspoon Cajun seasoning (see right)
    2 tablespoons extra virgin olive oil
    2 tablespoons finely diced Tasso ham (available at specialty markets)
    2 tablespoons shredded pickled pork or shredded smoked pork-shoulder butt
    3 tablespoons diced yellow onion
    3 tablespoons diced red onion
    2 tablespoons thinly sliced green onion, white and green parts
    2 teaspoons roasted garlic puree
    1 cup diced green pepper
   ⅓ cup diced celery
    2 teaspoons seeded and minced jalapeño pepper
   ¼ teaspoon Hungarian paprika
   ¼ teaspoon Spanish paprika
   ⅛ teaspoon chili powder
   ⅛ teaspoon freshly ground black pepper
   ⅛ teaspoon ground white pepper
   ⅛ teaspoon crushed red pepper flakes
   ⅛ teaspoon Worcestershire sauce
   ⅛ teaspoon hot pepper sauce
    1 small bay leaf
  1½ cups chicken stock
  one 5½-ounce can tomato sauce
  1½ teaspoons blond roux
    1 pound rock shrimp or other small shrimp, cooked and peeled
    2 tablespoons unsalted butter, chilled and cut into small pieces

For the Cajun seasoning

    3 tablespoons Hungarian paprika
  1½ tablespoons Spanish paprika
    5 teaspoons salt
  1¼ teaspoons dried thyme
  1¼ teaspoons dried oregano
    1 teaspoon ground white pepper
   ½ teaspoon dried basil
   ½ teaspoon cayenne pepper
   ¼ teaspoon freshly ground black pepper
   ⅛ teaspoon garlic powder
   ⅛ teaspoon onion powder

Cook the orzo according to the directions on package. Season the chicken with 1 tablespoon of the cajun seasoning.

In a large, heavy-bottomed Dutch oven (preferably enameled cast iron), heat the olive oil over high heat. When the oil is hot but not smoking, add the chicken and brown it for 5 minutes, stirring frequently. Add the ham and pork and cook for 2 more minutes. Stir in the three kinds of onions and the garlic puree and cook for an additional 2 minutes. Add the green pepper, celery, jalapeño, Hungarian and Spanish paprikas, chili powder, black and white peppers, red pepper flakes, Worcestershire sauce, hot pepper sauce, bay leaf, and remaining ¼ teaspoon cajun seasoning. Mix thoroughly to coat the meat and vegetables with the seasonings.

Pour in the chicken stock and tomato sauce and bring to a boil. Reduce the heat to medium-low and simmer, uncovered, for 50 minutes. Whisk in the blond roux, add the shrimp, and cook for 5 minutes to heat through. Add the butter, then stir in the cooked orzo and serve.

Jorge Rodriguez

Jorge Rodriguez named his restaurant, the Chimichurri Grill, after the pungent, green parsley-garlic-vinegar sauce that is the national condiment of Argentina. To be honest, it looks like something from a Doctor Seuss book, but it tastes so good—especially Jorge's version, which is tangy with a hint of heat underneath. I heard about the Chimichurri Grill from David Rosengarten, a journalist who writes for many food and wine magazines and knows all the good places off the beaten track. When I saw the address on Ninth Avenue and 43rd Street in Manhattan, I figured it was one of the small ethnic joints that fill the neighborhood known as Hell's Kitchen, but it far exceeded my expectations. The restaurant sits right on the corner underneath a simple neon sign. It's a tiny storefront, seating only thirty-six diners at a time. Candles on each table give the room a warm, romantic glow that's reflected in wood-framed mirrors hung on the walls. The white tablecloths are spotless and the waiters wear black pants, starched white shirts, and long white aprons folded over at the top. The atmosphere is simple, sophisticated, and intimate. Diners sit elbow-to-elbow, and it was very inviting to see entrées on other tables before we had to choose our own.

One dish that stood out was an appetizer that looked like a regular omelet—spicy eggs, potatoes, and chorizo sausages—that Jorge later explained was a frittata. At another table was a skirt steak, served still smoking from the grill, topped with the green chimichurri sauce. This didn't help us make up our minds, so when the waiter came over we admitted that we had no idea what to order. Usually a waiter responds by launching into the day's specials, but he said, "I'll be right back," and disappeared into the tiny narrow kitchen in the back. Out came a man with his chef's jacket open at the collar, who greeted us with, "I'm Jorge (pronounced hor-hay), the owner. Let me tell you a little about our food." He had no idea where I worked, and as the night went on I saw him greet many other new diners the same way, even though there were probably only two other cooks in the back. Sometimes chefs can give you the impression that you'd better take off and do your homework, but Jorge's attitude was just the opposite.

Each of Jorge's dishes has a history behind it. Right off the bat he told us we had to start with his grandmother's frittata. As a little boy in Buenos Aires, he and his family would eat a frittata at the end of every week that was full of the leftovers from Monday and Tuesday and Wednesday. He didn't like onions, so his grandmother would make him his own personal frittata without the onions—though the restaurant version sticks to his grandmother's recipe. He prides himself on his empanadas, pastry crust filled with ground beef, olives, raisins, cumin, and hard-boiled egg, or oxtail with onion marmalade. If these dishes sound European, it's because the population of Argentina is more European than mestizo or Indian, and Italian and Spanish settlers have had an enormous influence on the country's cuisine.

We also enjoyed a collard green soup with beans and chorizo sausage and potatoes. I smiled, thinking of collard greens as strictly a North American soul food item, but Jorge set me straight. He even grew up with the collards his grandmother grew in her backyard. I tasted each of the four simple ingredients in the soup very clearly. Jorge also cooks some of the best *pommes frites* in Manhattan—he slices them really thin and fries them to perfection, seasoning them with sea salt and garlic. Although they're not Argentinean, when you eat them with the beef, your taste buds are happy.

Though you can get empanadas with chard and cheese, vegetarians eating at Chimichurri Grill are really missing out since beef is probably the most notable Argentine staple. It comes from free-range cattle that graze on the pampas, the rich grasslands of central Argentina. The result is a lean low-cholesterol meat with the richest beef flavor in the world. Jorge suggested the juicy skirt steak grilled between slices of eggplant and zucchini or the fatty short ribs, a cut like spareribs, marinated in chimichurri sauce and grilled over a low heat. Whether the main dish is steak, organ meats, vegetables, or fish—Argentines eat a good deal of seafood too—grilling is definitely the cooking method of choice in Argentina. Finally I settled on the skirt steak, the meat had a soft, buttery texture and a wonderful earthy taste. The neon Chimichurri sauce added flair to the dish.

We had one glass of wine with the appetizer and a second with our entrée, and both perfectly complimented the food. Jorge is the sommelier. The wine list is in his head, and he not only tells you the name of the wine and what kind of food it goes with, but where the vineyard is located and the history of the people who grow the grapes and make the wine. Jorge wanted to introduce New Yorkers to Argentinean cuisine, and he's broadened that mission to include the wines of his country, which are relatively inexpensive and very good. Every year he is invited back to Argentina by the beef and wine purveyors, and he tours the country to make sure he's doing justice to the cuisine of the country as a whole.

Jorge was born in Argentina's capital city, Buenos Aires. He loved American music, and when he was eighteen he came to the United States to go to Woodstock and never returned. He loved playing the congas and started working in Manhattan's underground clubs. Even now, when he closes up shop around 1 A.M., the urge to play sometimes kicks in. It's not unusual to see him up on stage with a borrowed set of congas at Babalou, a nearby Spanish restaurant that turns into a club after midnight, and you'd never know he just put in an eighteen-hour day. But after taking a job in an Italian restaurant, Jorge began to doubt his plan to make a go of it as a musician. He had grown up watching his grandmother cook for his extended family and found cooking deeply satisfying. After ten years as a line cook he decided to visit Italy to experience the country and cuisine firsthand.

He got a two-week position working with chef Gian Paulo Belloni in Genoa. It turned into the gig of a lifetime because the Pope happened to be visiting the region at the time, and he got to make a "celestial dinner" for the pontiff. Yet on his way back to his old job in New York City, Jorge realized Italian food wasn't a cuisine he could ever consider his own. He started saving up, and four years later he opened the Chimichurri Grill. Hell's Kitchen wasn't as trendy then, and he chose it because it was affordable.

The grill got two little write-ups in local papers, and Ruth Reichl, the city's premier food critic at the time, must have seen one of them, because she walked in the first Thursday Jorge was officially open for business. He wasn't feeling quite ready for prime time and was terribly nervous, but he jumped into the kitchen. The next day in her column, Reichl essentially gave

Chimichurri her blessing as the "simultaneously sophisticated and homelike" place to get authentic Argentinean cuisine.

Jorge's food has nothing to do with formal culinary training. And he's not one of those chefs who feels obliged to reinvent or improve upon a regional cuisine. He makes the most of what Argentinean cuisine has to offer. It's home cooking, and as Reichl said, "distinctive food, lovingly cooked." This is Jorge's soul food. He devised his menu by remembering the foods of his childhood, and when he makes his annual trip back to Argentina, he builds on those memories.

Jorge may not be a household name, but he's not looking to set up a chain, or seeking an investor to bankroll a sixty-five seat venue. He commutes from New Jersey, where he has a wife and three kids, and he tries hard to balance work and family life. That isn't easy when you're as involved in the day-to-day operations as Jorge is. Another chef once told him that you know when you've really arrived when you can make love to your wife and think about the next day's special at the same time and not loose focus on either. Jorge's wife may not love the analogy, but the great chefs like Jorge live in a world of their own, where food is never far from their thoughts.

Traveling Squab with Cabbage

Makes 6 servings

3 tablespoons olive oil
6 squabs, cleaned and cut in half lengthwise

For the cabbage
2 medium onions, thinly sliced
1 large carrot, chopped
4 garlic cloves, minced
3 tablespoons minced fresh parsley, leaves only
3 ounces finely chopped pancetta

1 head savoy cabbage (about 1½ pounds), carefully washed and cut in narrow strips
12 dried juniper berries, crushed
1 teaspoon ground thyme
2 tablespoons fresh rosemary leaves
½ teaspoon ground cumin
1 tablespoon sweet paprika
½ teaspoon caraway seeds
Kosher salt or coarse sea salt
12 whole black peppercorns
2 green apples, sliced
1 cup red wine
1 tablespoon flour
¼ cup sour cream
6 sprigs fresh rosemary, for garnish

Brown the squabs in the olive oil in a heavy flame-proof casserole over medium heat. When brown on both sides, remove the birds and set them aside.

Place the onions in the casserole and sauté until golden. Add the carrots, garlic, parsley, and pancetta and sauté for few minutes more, then add the cabbage. Continue cooking, stirring to combine, until the cabbage is slightly brown and wilted. Add the juniper berries, thyme, rosemary, cumin, paprika, caraway seeds, salt to taste, and peppercorns. Stir in the apple slices and the wine and bring the cabbage mixture to a boil.

Toast the flour in a hot skillet without oil until it is light brown. Sprinkle the toasted flour over the cabbage mixture and stir to combine. Reduce the heat to low and return the squabs to the casserole.

Cover the casserole tightly and simmer for 20 minutes. Transfer the cabbage mixture to a serving platter and top with the squab halves. Spoon a dollop of sour cream on each portion, garnish with a sprig of rosemary, and serve.

Gail and Anthony Uglesich

On my thirtieth birthday my fiancé and I headed to New Orleans with our good friends and mentors Lou and Terri Latilla, who were really excited about our plan to eat our way through the city. My actual birthday dinner was to be at Emeril's, and I asked him where else to eat during our visit. "There's a place on the outskirts of the Garden District," he answered. "It's not fancy, but it serves some of the best down-home cooking in New Orleans, and my friend Anthony and his wife Gail will really make you feel at home. It's called Uglesich's."

I believed Emeril when he said they didn't take reservations, but did not heed his advice to show up for lunch by ten-thirty in the morning. When we pulled up at 11:15 A.M. outside a beat-up building on a rundown corner, there were easily sixty people already in line—including the mayor. Fortunately the line moves fairly fast, winding through low slightly rickety French doors into an undistinguished pine-paneled room and past a makeshift bar. That's where you place your order; there's only one waitress. A sweet-looking gray-haired man stands at the counter scribbling orders. When we finally reached him, I said, "You must be Anthony. Emeril suggested we eat here." Brightening at the mention of Emeril's name, he led us to a table at the back, and handed us his laminated menu. He was giving us the chance to try something that caught our eye, but said he'd prefer to send out some of his specialties.

My fiancé stuck with the fried fish platter, which bore the name "Paul's Fantasy" and consisted of a pan-fried trout filet covered with grilled shrimp and crispy new potatoes. I took the opportunity to ask Anthony all kinds of questions about the catch of the day, what made his sauces so special, and what was in the Shrimp Uggie. (It turned out to be sautéed shrimp and potatoes served with a fire-engine-red sauce the Uglesichs make with hot sauce, ketchup, and vegetable oil.) Anthony suggested oysters, sautéed in the shell. Anthony's barbecue sauce combines garlic, Worcestershire sauce, and lemon; the ingredients are standard but somehow the sauce is not. He claims, "It's all in the mix, baby."

The barbecued oysters came out first, followed by the Shrimp Uggie delivered by Anthony himself. It's the kind of place where dishes appear whenever they're ready, and you dig in immediately. Next came the crabmeat and potato platter, which consists of a cake that combines crabmeat, potatoes, onions, and Egg Beaters, which apparently hold the dish together nicely—it's not a cholesterol-cutting move. The other mystery ingredients are seasonings the Uglesichs describe coyly as "the regular New Orleans spices." The only ingredients they'll divulge are salt, pepper, and cayenne. The Catfish Italiana, dipped in olive oil then coated with a breadcrumb and imported cheese mixture and sautéed with fresh lemon juice squeezed on top, was a welcome departure from the

standard fried or blackened catfish. The dish had a nice heat and the tomato gave it a fresh sweet bite. The Firecracker Shrimp were sautéed barbecue sauce containing Asian and Creole ingredients topped with horseradish cream. We wrapped up with their etouffée, crayfish smothered with onions, bell peppers, garlic, and celery, served over white rice.

The menu at Uglesich's says right up front, "We serve no desserts and no coffee." Given the line outside and the state of our stomachs, we understood why. When I told Anthony how glad we were to have made his restaurant one of our stops, he put his arm around me and gave me a kiss on the forehead. The next time I came by I met Miss Gail, as Anthony's wife is known. Gail spends most of her time behind the scenes creating and testing new dishes, but she can sometimes be found out front taking orders with Anthony. She may not be as boisterous as her husband, but she works just as hard, and she clearly moves things along at the restaurant.

The restaurant is only open for lunch, and Gail heads home at 4 P.M. and Anthony at 6 P.M. Descended from Croatian immigrants, Sam Uglesich, Anthony's father, opened the first Uglesich's in the South Ramport district of New Orleans, and moved to the present location on Baronne Street in 1924. Over the years, the neighborhood has become somewhat dilapidated, and the aging home of Uglesich's blends right in. In fact, when the exterior got a paint job during the 80s, it made headlines in the local paper.

Sam kept the menu simple, making a name for Uglesich's with his fried oysters, shrimp, and trout. He also made po' boys, the classic New Orleans sandwich of fried fresh-shucked oysters or trout served on a roll dressed with lettuce, tomato, mayonnaise, and typically doused with hot sauce. And his fried egg sandwiches were famous. It's the quality of the food, not the ambience, that keeps diners lined up all week.

Anthony attended Louisiana State University, served in the military, and eventually returned to New Orleans where he met Gail on a blind date. They were married in 1963. When Sam got too old to keep up with the business, Anthony didn't want it to fall by the wayside. Gail was willing to leave her job as an elementary school teacher, so in 1966 they took over the restaurant.

It was Anthony and Gail's idea to add some classic New Orleans dishes to the menu. They agreed that Anthony would stay in the restaurant while Gail conducted her own food research, buying cookbooks, taking notes, and tasting the other gumbos, sauces, and etouffées served around town. She started trying and testing on her own, so that when Anthony came home he'd find new dishes lined up for him to try. He'd sample her roue, her gator stew (the menu says, "It won't snap back"), and her dirty rice (she adds white rice to the standard wild rice to improve the texture). After they agreed that a dish was ready, Anthony would start serving it in the restaurant.

Gail gets up every morning at four so she can start the cooking at home. At 10 A.M. Anthony loads up the van and brings the sauces and gumbos, the crab cake mixture, the rémoulade, and many other dishes into the restaurant. Gail arrives at 10:30 A.M. to help Anthony take orders. Anthony prides himself on being an expert fryer, with the perfect blend of seasonings and oil at just the right temperature. Although they work longer hours during the annual New Orleans Jazzfest, Uglesich's is only open five days a week and one Saturday a month. But even on the weekend, Gail and Anthony are thinking, planning, and working over the stove.

Asked when they have time for each other, Gail responds, "Anthony and I depend on each other—and we love what we do. People can eat at a lot of places in New Orleans, but we just want to cook food that makes them happy when they eat here." When Anthony turns sixty-five, the Uglesichs say they're going to retire. They've resisted offers to expand because they don't want to lose their product or themselves, and they'd rather close shop than put the business in the hands of someone who doesn't understand their way of doing things. Given the chance, they'd do it all over again.

Shrimp Uggie

Makes 4 servings

For the sauce
3 cups vegetable oil
2 cups ketchup
½ bottle (5 ounces) hot sauce or to taste
2 tablespoons fresh lemon juice
2 tablespoons salt
2 teaspoons fresh chopped parsley
2 teaspoons paprika
4 teaspoons crushed red pepper or to taste

1 to 1½ pounds medium shrimp, peeled and deveined
4 boiled new potatoes for garnish, optional

To make the sauce, combine all the ingredients and stir well. The sauce will keep for up to 3 weeks if refrigerated in an airtight container. When ready to use, stir again and scoop from the bottom of the container.

Put the desired amount of sauce in a skillet over medium-high heat and add the shrimp, tossing to coat. Sauté until the shrimp turn pink, 3 to 5 minutes. Serve hot with new potatoes for garnish, if desired.

Sam Choy

One of the first things I ever said to Sam Choy was, "Sam, we can buy another fish." This was in the spring of 1999, and Sam had flown to New York City to appear on the Food Network with Emeril and promote his new cookbook. He had insisted on bringing a Hawaiian fish called mahi mahi with him, but the fish hadn't made the connection in Los Angeles. Sam gives off the vibe of a person who never has a bad day. It's enough to make you want to move to Hawaii, but at that point he was looking pretty dejected. I told him that we could go to the fish market and find a substitute, but Sam really wanted to show Emeril and our New York City audience what the waters of Hawaii had to offer. In a final attempt to track down the missing mahi mahi, he went into the green room and started working the phone: "It's a fish. It's packed in ice. I'm at the Food Network. We're going live in an hour." Usually we supply the props, but when the mahi mahi arrived from JFK Airport thirty minutes before show time I realized we couldn't have gotten this fish. It weighed one hundred and fifty pounds, and it was as big as a couch. When this animated man in a Hawaiian shirt walked out carrying this huge fish and roared, "Aloha!" the audience went crazy. He prepared deep-fried mahi mahi macadamia nut fingers with Emeril, and the audi-

ence ate their performance up. And without the enormous fish, the show wouldn't have turned out as well as it did.

Sam was the ultimate guest, full of surprises with a personality that the audience really warmed up to. Although I'd been to Hawaii, I didn't truly understand the aloha spirit until I met Sam. He learned traditional Hawaiian cooking from his mother, who was half Hawaiian and half German. But his Chinese father was the family cook, and he taught his son what Sam refers to as "the secrets of Oriental cuisine." The family business was organizing luaus—a luau is a party that celebrates the history of Hawaii—for eight hundred tourists every weekend. They served traditional dishes such as pig roasted in an underground pit, pil (finely chopped purple taro root), and a tapestry of local fruits and delicacies: pineapples, bananas, coconuts, Asian pears, and macadamia nuts. Traditional music and dancing accompany the feast. Sam grew up listening to his father talking about the joy of food and how it could be used to teach people about Hawaii.

Sam was a star football player, but he gave it up after high school to go to cooking school on the Big Island. After graduation he worked in several prestigious hotels and developed something of a following. His ambition was to get people to realize that Hawaiian cuisine was much more than tourist food or the sampling of classic dishes served at a luau. In 1991 he opened up Sam Choy's in an industrial part of Kona, the only area he could afford. Hawaiians have soul food, the food people eat day to day, and that's Sam's specialty. His first customers were truckers and secretaries from nearby businesses. Word of mouth has since earned Sam an international reputation, but the clientele is still predominantly local. Since few people are in the area at night, the only meals served at this Sam Choy's are breakfast and lunch, and the place closes at 2 P.M.

After his visit to New York City I'd put Sam on something of a pedestal, and when I arrived in Kona, I couldn't help thinking, "Wow, this is it?" The restaurant is approximately five miles from the airport, and you have to make an effort to get there. It's a square white building, with industrial glass doors that open into a big room with an open kitchen, a cashier's desk on the left, and tables full of families, truckers, and fellow tourists. There's great Hawaiian art on the wall but that's as fancy as it gets.

The plates may not match and presentation may not be a top priority, but the food is incredible. A big thing in Hawaii is the plate lunch, which is like a blue-plate special, consisting of a heaping helping of comfort food: steak sashimi, fried chicken and crab, short ribs. Barbecuing is popular on the islands, and Sam makes a plate with shredded barbecued pork on the side (Hawaiian barbecue sauce is very sweet and fruity), accompanied by shrimp-topped salad served with papaya dressing. He serves moi moi saimin, kakimochi wasabi crusted island fish with shoyu butter (shoyu is a kind of soy sauce). On an East Coast menu, that might translate into something like a horseradish-crusted halibut with tropical salsa. He does macadamia nut crusted pork loin and coconut curried shrimp, along with his own "Big Aloha" brew. I know of no other chef who'd serve Spam, but Hawaiians eat a lot of it and Sam makes a double-decker sandwich of shrimp tempura with teriyaki beef, spinach, Vienna sausages, and chunks of Spam. That's how authentically local his menu is.

Most chefs embrace different philosophies about the food they cook, but Sam just talks about bringing simple ingredients from the sea or the garden into the kitchen. He brings each dish to the next level, though. People don't just say "Go to Sam's."

They recommend specific things like the steamed mahi mahi luau pork tofu, which is an extraordinary blend of flavors and textures in a single dish. The mahi mahi and the pork are common fare, but the tofu is a twist added by Sam. His beef stew is a must, even in the heat of August. The meat comes from a cattle ranch called Hulapollakula, located in Maui's "up country." In Hawaii, poke is considered a poor man's fish, like catfish. It's traditionally eaten nearly raw, sprinkled on salads, but Sam decided to toss it in the wok with seaweed and sesame. He now sells over a thousand pounds a week of fried poke, which has become his signature dish.

Today Sam has a flagship restaurant in Diamond Head that specializes in Hawaiian regional cuisine, featuring fresh fish of the day. Sam Choy's Diamond Head is also home to Sam's cooking show, "Sam Choy's Kitchen." Opened in Honolulu in 1997, Sam Choy's Breakfast, Lunch, and Crab is more of a family restaurant, popular for its Alaskan King Crab legs and generous "Sam-sized" portions. Also included in the restaurant is a brewery called Sam Choy's Big Aloha Brewery. Sam's on Maui, Sam's in Guam, and Sam Choy's in Tokyo and San Diego offer Sam's creative Hawaiian fare in somewhat more formal settings.

I'm sure he's been approached by a lot of businessmen to take his operation upscale, but Sam insists on running a casual place where people can wear shorts and T-shirts and everyone feels comfortable. Those are the people who come up and greet him on the street, proud of this local boy who put Hawaiian food on the map. He knows that there's a lot more to Hawaii than waterfalls and surfing, and that this side of the islands can be experienced through food: heavenly Hawaiian coffee from Kona, aged Hawaiian Vintage Chocolate, fish cakes from little Erna's truck stop down on the road, where Erna's husband probably did the fishing and she was up at dawn making the batter.

His father died a few years ago, after getting to see Sam open two of his places. Sam has worked hard at keeping his father's love of Hawaiian cooking alive and becoming one of Hawaii's premier chefs. The islands have a unique mix of food and culture, and Sam has become their proud ambassador.

■■ ■ ■■ ■

South Pacific Lobster and Seafood Salad with Honey- and Macadamia Nut–Crusted Banana

Makes two main-course servings

For the poaching liquid
2 cups water
1 cup white wine
½ cup diced carrots
½ cup diced onions
½ cup diced celery
  Juice of ½ lemon
½ teaspoon salt
¼ teaspoon cracked pepper

Fill a pot with the above ingredients and bring to a boil. Reduce the heat to a simmer and completely submerge the 2 cups lobster meat and 1 pound shrimp (see salad ingredients below) in the poaching water. Cover and cook gently at a low simmer until pink. Make sure not to overcook the seafood!

For the banana garnish
4 apple or finger bananas, peeled
½ cup honey
½ cup chopped, macadamia nuts, toasted

Dip the whole bananas in the honey and roll in the macadamia nuts. Refrigerate until serving time.

For the lobster and seafood salad
2 cups poached lobster meat (see poaching recipe above)
2 cups lump crabmeat
1 pound extra-large shrimp (16 to 20), poached, peeled, and deveined (see poaching recipe above)
3 ounces minced Maui onion or other sweet onion
3 tablespoons minced celery
1 medium bell pepper, minced
½ cup pitted and sliced black olives
1 cup chopped fresh spinach, sautéed in olive oil and squeezed dry (about 1 cup cooked)
4 boiled eggs, sliced
1½ cups diced, cooked yams
½ cup sweet peas
1 cup sliced water chestnuts
½ teaspoon curry powder
½ teaspoon chopped fresh dill
½ teaspoon salt
1 teaspoon black pepper
1½ cups homemade or store-bought mayonnaise
two large, round sourdough loaves

Here we go! In a large mixing bowl, add all of the salad ingredients. Gently fold all the ingredients together and make sure to add a lot of TLC (that's tender, loving care). Cover the salad and refrigerate to chill.

Hollow out the sourdough loaves, saving the tops to serve as covers. (The soft bread removed from the interiors can be used as breadcrumbs later.) Divide the salad between the two bread bowls. Add two of the honey- and nut-crusted bananas and top with the reserved bread covers. Enjoy!

AFTERWORD

I first met Rochelle in 1994, when she dined at the kitchen table of my restaurant in Chicago. One of her dinner companions that evening was Alan Lowenfeld who had brought along an unusual utensil called the "Extendafork" that he had been demonstrating earlier that day at the annual Chicago housewares trade-show. As its name implies, the Extendafork, when lengthened, allows the user to eat from other people's plates with ease. Rochelle, extremely amused by the fork, used it jokingly at certain times throughout the evening to sample food from across the table. Because she made using the Extendafork look like such fun, I ended up ordering two dozen to have on hand at the restaurant.

In contrast to the laughs we had over the fork, when each dish arrived at the table Rochelle took the time to study it carefully. She had an intense curiosity about the dishes and asked questions about specific ingredients. After speaking with her for only a few minutes, I became aware that she was not only intelligent, but also extremely ambitious to learn about food. At that point I knew she was going to be successful in her career at the Food Network.

What distinguishes Rochelle in the food world is that her passion goes beyond the food on the table to the people behind the stove. She realizes that not every great chef has graduated from culinary school, grown up in a restaurant family, aspires to own more than one restaurant, or wants to cook four-star cuisine. Rochelle knows that food is a vehicle for telling stories, and she has gathered the stories of twenty diverse and talented chefs, which she shares here. As a chef, I have the opportunity to meet wonderful people from all walks of life, but it is rare to meet one with the sheer passion for food, wine, and people that Rochelle has.

Charlie Trotter

Charlie Trotter

What was your worst disaster in the kitchen? Taking myself too seriously

Who was your biggest celebrity dinner guest? Cooking for Emeril Lagasse—it still makes me nervous!

If you could eat only one thing for the rest of your life what would it be? 1900 Chateaux Margaux

Is there an ingredient/food that you always steer clear of? Rattle snake—I cannot imagine touching one or eating one!

Would you prefer to cook for one person or 100? One—the one I love

How often do you cook at home? Whenever I can, which is not too often

If you weren't a chef what would your occupation be? A writer—writing about food and wine

Do you ever eat junk food or other foods that would surprise us? Yes, Häagen-Dazs by the pint!

What is your most creative/elaborate dish and/or biggest flop? Every day I try to simplify, simplify, simplify.

Who is your favorite person to cook for? My Mom

What is your favorite city in which to dine? Chicago, of course

What is your favorite childhood memory involving food? Making Mad Hatter Meatballs from the *Alice in Wonderland Cookbook*

Emeril Lagasse

What was your worst disaster in the kitchen? I haven't really had any major disasters, but one time I was making an upside-down cake with peaches at the home of my dear friends, Jim and Betsy Fifield in Aspen, Colorado. I forgot to adjust my recipe to the high altitude and the whole thing blew up! All I can say is…when in doubt, there's always ice cream.

Who were your biggest celebrity dinner guests? As a young man, I was very involved with music. I had been offered a full music scholarship to college, but I made the decision to work my way through cooking school. What has been absolutely great about the path I chose is that over the years several music people have come back into my life through food. It's been a pleasure to cook for Billy Joel, Jimmy Buffet, Sammy Hagar, and Don Henley.

But I wouldn't be doing any justice to only mention musicians. I'd be leaving lots of friends out… Andre Agassi and Robin Williams are two that immediately come to mind. It's also culinary challenging but always very rewarding to cook for your colleagues—Julia Child, Charlie Trotter, Daniel Boulud, Roger Vergé, and Norman Van Aken are some of my favorites. Moreso than celebrity status, it just makes me feel great to make anyone happy with food.

If you could eat only one thing for the rest of your life, what would it be? I would eat pasta. It's so versatile—there are countless things you can do with it.

Is there an ingredient/food you always steer clear of? I'm into real food—fresh ingredients and simplicity. I tend to stay away from ingredients that are weird…rattlesnake comes to mind.

Would you prefer to cook for one person or 100? I truly enjoy both, but there's something romantic about cooking for just one other special person. Certainly the cleanup is easier.

How often do you cook at home? As often as possible. These days I prefer eating at home more than eating out. I've tried to instill the importance of a strong family table. I believe you have to make time for family time and family dining, particularly on weekends (my favorite day being Sundays).

What is the most romantic dinner you ever cooked? Most dinners that I cook are for my wife, the kids, and/or with family and friends. I think that food can be as sexual or romantic as you make it. My motto whenever I cook is always "food of love."

Lidia Bastianich

What are your favorite places to visit (and eat) when you're in Italy? My favorite places to visit when in Italy are the local, regional fruit and vegetable markets with the farmers who bring their seasonal products in for sale. Sometimes they have a stall, and sometimes their goods are piled up on an inverted wooden crate or in their trunks. I get the simplest and best recipes from these farmers. In addition, I always pay a visit to the local butchers, bakers, and fish markets.

What's the biggest difference between Italian and Italian-American cooking? Both cuisines are born of Italian culture and are miles apart in their execution, preparation, and taste. The Italian American cuisine is a cuisine of adaptation; it had its genesis in the late 1800s/beginning of the 1900s when the first large influx of Italian immigrants came to the United States. They brought with them their culinary heritage but there was no olive oil, Parmigiano Reggiano, San Marzano tomatoes. Therefore, they had to adapt to the available products. Much more garlic was used, as was more meat; and sauces cooked for longer times.

What is your family's most requested dish from you? The adults love risotto with lobster while the grandchildren ask for gnocchi with Parmigiano Reggiano.

Who was your all-time favorite dinner guest? My all-time favorite dinner guest has got to be Julia Child. She is very simple in her demands and yet very expressive and direct in her comments and praises. Her favorite dish of mine was risotto with mushrooms.

If you could eat only one thing for the rest of your life what would it be? Pasta...you can turn anything into a condiment for pasta and make it a great and satisfying dish.

Would you prefer to cook for one person or 100? Neither is optimal. Cooking for six to twelve people is ideal for me. There is enough product interaction to reach optimal levels of flavor and texture and six to twelve people means that you will have a great table for conversation and enjoyment.

How often do you cook at home? Whenever I am home, I cook. This means that it usually happens on weekends when we have four generations at the table.

If you weren't a chef what would your occupation be? Pediatrician

Daniel Boulud

Who were your biggest celebrity dinner guests? Dustin Hoffman, Robin Williams, Whoopi Goldberg, Woody Allen, Bill Clinton, and Bill Cosby

If you could eat only one thing for the rest of your life what would it be? DB Burger: The burger is composed of an exterior of ground sirloin with a filling of boned short ribs braised in red wine, foie gras, black truffle, and a mirepoix of root vegetables. The homemade bun is topped with toasted Parmesan and layered with fresh horseradish mayonnaise, tomato confit, fresh tomato, and frisée lettuce. Can you say that in one breath?

Is there an ingredient/food that you always steer clear of? Bananas. I just don't like them.

Would you prefer to cook for one person or 100? For 100—spread the pleasure.

How often do you cook at home? On Sundays...when I can.

If you weren't a chef what would your occupation be? What else is there?

What is the most romantic dinner you ever cooked? It was a dinner in Hong Kong for my wife, Micky's birthday. At the Hong Kong Market, I found ingredients I had never encountered before, and it was a joy to use them to create an unexpectedly surprising meal for Micky and our friends.

Do you ever eat junk food or other foods that would surprise us? Fruit Roll-ups, licorice sticks, bubble gum, Krispy Kreme donuts and Popeye's fried chicken

What is your most creative dish? The DB Burger... see above!

What was your biggest flop? I lost a truck shipment of 800 gourmet picnic baskets for guests boarding an airplane to Morocco to attend Malcolm Forbes's birthday party. It took the army, the air force, the CIA, and the National Guard, but we did eventually find the truck, and the meal was served.

Who is your favorite person to cook for? A noted chef who is a friend and who will challenge me to my outer limits to please him or her.

What is your favorite city in which to dine? New York City, bien sûr!

Marcus Samuelsson

What was your worst disaster in the kitchen? When I was working at a restaurant in Switzerland, the menus were in French, the meetings were in German, neither language of which I completely understood, so I missed parts of both languages, and I was thinking in Swedish. It was disastrous.

Who were your biggest celebrity dinner guests?
Paul McCartney and Bill Clinton; however my favorite guests are the ones who return again and again because they are the ones who allow a restaurant to survive.

If you could eat only one thing for the rest of your life what would it be? Sushi

Would you prefer to cook for one person or 100? 15 or 20 at this level—one isn't much fun.

How often do you cook at home? Once a week, on Sunday

If you weren't a chef what would your occupation be?
Pastry chef or baker

What is the most romantic dinner you ever cooked? When I was still in Sweden, I cooked for a girl at home, and we started to fight because I was interested in making all of this weird food, but she just wanted to hang out.

Do you ever eat junk food or other foods that would surprise us?
Miso soup, not all food that is fast has to be bad food.

Who is your favorite person to cook for? My mom because she doesn't see me as a chef, she sees me just as Marcus.

What is your favorite city in which to dine? New York City, Paris, Tokyo, and Singapore

What is your favorite childhood memory involving food? I have great memories from Christmastime because my mom and grandmother began preparing the traditional Swedish Christmas table in October.

Rick Bayless

If you could eat only one thing for the rest of your life what would it be? Corn tortillas because I wrap so many different things in them

Is there an ingredient/food that you always steer clear of? Tomato juice makes me gag.

Would you prefer to cook for one person or 100? When cooking for one you can create a private, intimate magic while cooking for 100 is a different kind of magic because it's a party-like festive atmosphere. I hope that I can continue to cook for both for the rest of my life because they are so different.

How often do you cook at home? Three to four times a week— breakfast is our family meal together.

If you weren't a chef what would your occupation be? Writer, actor, or painter

Do you ever eat junk food or other foods that would surprise us?
Fried dough—funnel cakes and doughnuts

Who is your favorite person to cook for? My wife and daughter because when we get together it's communal—we each contribute a dish.

What is your favorite childhood memory involving food? Every summer at my grandma's we would pick peaches in the orchard and over the next several days we would pickle and can them and make butter and jam to last throughout the entire year.

Norman Van Aken

Would you prefer to cook for one person or 100? One person if it was someone I loved but if it were a group where I knew no one I'd cook for 100. I am a chef because I love to share my passion and that means sharing it with as many people as I can.

How often do you cook at home? Once about every three weeks. Our restaurant is closed on Sundays, but there are many Sundays we are doing charity events and traveling around the country that I don't get to cook at home as much as I'd like just yet.

If you weren't a chef what would your occupation be? I would probably be a writer. I'd specialize in food and travel writing I'm sure. If I had the talent I would have been a blues musician. My son might be the first in our family to be in the music business though. One other love I'd try to explore is teaching small children more about food and healthy eating.

What was the most romantic meal you ever cooked? The most romantic meal I cooked was a breakfast. I decided to splurge and go all out and have a fancy dinner at a restaurant well beyond my means on the occasion of the nineteenth birthday of Janet, my future wife. At that time I was working the graveyard shift at a barbecue called the Midget in Key West. After the dinner I had to go to work. We walked there together and just as I was going to kiss her goodbye we learned that the guy that was supposed to work with me doing the dishes was a no show. Without a moment's hesitation Janet put on an apron and a bandana and helped me all through the night washing the pots and dishes while I grilled ribs and burgers for the late night revelers. We walked home exhausted just as the sun was coming up. When we got to our little cottage I cooked her an omelet. It wasn't fancy but I fed it to her while she lay in a hammock before falling into a deep sleep.

What is your most creative dish? Well certainly one of them is my Down Island French Toast. It seems to be one of the dishes that really rocks my chef friends and people who travel and have eaten foie gras in many forms. My buddy Emeril Lagasse has made it both in his restaurants and on his television show. He makes a version that I might call "Texas French Toast" it's so BIG! I love that man.

Sara Moulton

What was your worst disaster in the kitchen? When I was working at La Tulipe (a 3-star restaurant in New York City) in the early 1980s and James Beard came in for dinner and I overcooked his rack of lamb. My boss, the executive chef, made me cook another, and James Beard had to wait forever.

Who was your biggest celebrity dinner guest? Julia Child

If you could eat only one thing for the rest of your life what would it be? Stinky cheese

Is there a food that you always steer clear of? Processed food—it just tastes artificial.

Would you prefer to cook for one person or 100? One—I can do it with more care.

How often do you cook at home? Five nights a week (no kidding!)

If you weren't a chef what would your occupation be? Special education or elementary school teacher

What is the most romantic dinner you ever cooked? Going out to dinner with my husband is more romantic for me. We both like all the hoopla—it makes us feel special.

Do you ever eat junk food or other foods that would surprise us? Potato chips

What is your most creative/elaborate dish and/or biggest flop? I am just a good cook, comfort food style. I can't say there is one dish I do better than another. Flops? I never attempt anything too wild, so don't get into too much trouble.

Who is your favorite person to cook for? My family

What is your favorite city in which to dine? New York City and Paris

What is your favorite childhood memory involving food? I have many—mostly cooking with my grandmother, Ruth, when I was very little—we made bread, cookies, and Johnny cakes.

Matthew Kenney

What was your worst disaster in the kitchen? In the middle of service one evening at Matthew's, the fire suppression system was accidentally tripped and activated, covering everything and everyone in the kitchen with white powder.

Who was your biggest celebrity dinner guest? Paul Bocuse

If you could eat only one thing for the rest of your life what would it be? Chocolate or cheese and bread, but I guess that's three.

Is there an ingredient/food that you always steer clear of? Garlic—about a year ago, I developed a sort of allergy and it upsets my stomach, even a small amount.

Would you prefer to cook for one person or 100? One person—so that I could focus on every detail and make it perfect.

How often do you cook at home? Two times per week

If you weren't a chef what would your occupation be? Architect

What is the most romantic dinner you ever cooked? The first dinner I cooked for my girlfriend during our first summer in our cottage in Maine—it was very simple, but the setting was idyllic.

Do you ever eat junk food or other foods that would surprise us? Not really—except chocolate, but I don't consider that junk food.

What is your most creative dish? Squab lasagna—sounded odd, but it was great—free-form lasagna with paper-thin sheets of pasta, squab cooked with ginger, game stock, scallions, and cilantro with shiitakes and yellow pepper.

Who is your favorite person to cook for? My girlfriend—we share almost identical tastes and so appreciate the same flavors and ingredients.

What is your favorite city in which to dine? Milan

What is your favorite childhood memory involving food? One summer in Maine we grew wild strawberries, and they were amazing.

Leah Chase

What was your worst disaster in the kitchen? It's a disaster when I walk into the restaurant and find that nobody else is there yet except me!

Who was your biggest celebrity dinner guest? Quincy Jones is my all-time favorite.

If you could eat only one thing for the rest of your life what would it be? Meatballs and spaghetti

Is there an ingredient/food that you always steer clear of? Cilantro—it's too overpowering.

Would you prefer to cook for one person or 100? I'd prefer to cook for 100. My extended family numbers around 200, and my mom raised eleven kids, so I'm more in the habit of cooking for large groups.

How often do you cook at home? Never—I'm never home! However, I do have a private dining room at Dooky Chase that I use for entertaining.

What is the most romantic dinner you ever cooked? When one of my grandsons becomes serious with a girl, I prepare what has become known as the "long table" dinner for them. It is a full course meal, served on a very long dining table complete with candlesticks. When the girlfriend gets invited for a "long table" dinner it is a sign that she's in.

Do you ever eat junk food or other foods that would surprise us? Potato chips and chocolate candy

Who is your favorite person to cook for? Anyone who enjoys food and isn't picky

What is your favorite city in which to dine? I've traveled all over the place and enjoy other types of food, but there's just no other place for eating like New Orleans.

What is your favorite childhood memory involving food? As a child I always looked forward to the meal on Sunday. During the week we would eat things such as string beans and rice—never anything with meat in it—and for Sunday dinner we would have a huge meal with everything from chicken and veal to macaroni and cheese to gumbo.

Todd English

Who was your biggest celebrity dinner guest? Julia Child

Is there an ingredient/food that you always steer clear of? Dill

How often do you cook at home? On the weekends with my kids—we go shopping for ingredients and then cook together.

If you weren't a chef what would your occupation be? Baseball player or professional golfer

Do you ever eat junk food or other foods that would surprise us? Cornnuts and McDonald's french fries

Who is your favorite person to cook for? My kids

What is your favorite city in which to dine? Palermo for the spleen sandwich at the Vuccheria, but nothing beats a New England clambake in Boston.

What is your favorite childhood memory involving food? Either making and drying pasta with my grandmother in Palermo or sitting in my uncle's bakery in the Bronx.

Bobby Flay

If you could eat only one thing for the rest of your life what would it be? I would eat a double Cheddar cheeseburger with grilled Vidalia onions and horseradish mustard.

How often do you cook at home? I try to cook at home at least once a week. In the winter, I like to prepare braised dishes that cook for hours, and in the summer I break out the grill at my summer home and grill everything possible.

Do you ever eat junk food or other foods that would surprise us? I don't know if it is surprising, but I always have a huge supply of Häagen-Dazs ice cream in my refrigerator at all times. It would have to be my favorite junk food.

What was your most creative dish or biggest flop? My most creative dish also turned out to be my biggest flop. When I opened Bolo, I decided that I was going to reinvent paella and created this elaborate version with duck. My business partners and friends all hated it and tried to convince me to take it off the menu before we got reviewed by the *New York Times*, but I wouldn't listen. I kept it on and Ruth Reichl totally blasted it in her review. Needless to say, I removed it from the menu the day that the review came out.

Who is your favorite person to cook for? My favorite person is my daughter. I love introducing her to new things and am always amazed that at six years of age, she already has a great palate.

What is your favorite city in which to dine? New York City. I travel a lot and have yet to find a place that has the amount of talent and great food that New York City has.

What is your favorite childhood memory involving food? Making sauerbraten with my grandmother. She was a great cook and is probably responsible for my interest in cooking.

Bernard Carmouche

If you could eat only one thing for the rest of your life what would it be? Fish

Is there an ingredient/food that you always steer clear of? Blue cheese because I don't like the smell or the taste of it!

What was your worst disaster in the kitchen? When the sprinkler heads burst in my meat cooker.

Would you prefer to cook for one person or 100? One or 100. You should treat all guests equally and show passion and love to all.

How often do you cook at home? Maybe once a week

If you weren't a chef what would your occupation be? Postman

What is the most romantic dinner you ever cooked? Maine lobster with truffles, for one of our guests at the kitchen table

Do you ever eat junk food or other foods that would surprise us? Yes—Lay's potato chips

What is your most creative/elaborate dish? Sea urchin & ahi tuna with truffle soy sauce

Who is your favorite person to cook for? Anyone who enjoys food and wine like I do

What is your favorite city in which to dine? New Orleans

What is your favorite childhood memory involving food? My mom's tuna with french fries

Allan Vernon

Who was your biggest celebrity dinner guest? Bill Cosby

What was your worst disaster in the kitchen? Opening day in 1982

If you could eat only one thing for the rest of your life what would it be? Fish

Is there an ingredient/food that you always steer clear of? MSG

Would you prefer to cook for one person or 100? 100, so I could see a lot of people looking happy.

How often do you cook at home? Once a week

If you weren't a chef what would your occupation be? Carpenter

What is the most romantic dinner you ever cooked? I made jerk shrimp and jerk salmon for my daughter's wedding.

What is your most creative dish? Jerk chicken

Who is your favorite person to cook for? My girlfriend, Yvonne Parker

What is your favorite city in which to dine? New York City

Michael Lomonaco

Who was your all-time favorite dinner guest? My favorite guest was Luciano Pavarotti, who came in full costume and make-up. I've also cooked for and met every president from Richard Nixon to Bill Clinton.

If you could eat only one thing for the rest of your life what would it be? A simple homemade pasta, enjoyed with my wife, Diane.

Would you prefer to cook for one person or 100? Cooking for 100 because it offers all the excitement of a Broadway opening.

How often do you cook at home? As frequently as time allows, given my work schedule. At least weekly—on my day off. I also cook at home during the holidays, if possible.

If you weren't a chef what would your occupation be? A filmmaker/director—to be creative and work in an ensemble atmosphere

What is the most romantic dinner you ever cooked? Cooking for my wife, Diane, on an average night—made special—with flowers, champagne, and her favorite foods.

Do you ever eat junk food or other foods that would surprise us? I never eat fast/chain food, but I love good homemade roadside cooking: fried chicken, ribs, and pies. And Ring Dings! Uh oh!

What is your favorite city in which to dine? New York City, for its wonderfully diverse ethnic mix, followed by Venice. How could you not love Venice?

What is your favorite childhood memory involving food? Coming home from grade school, doing my homework in the kitchen while watching my mother cook. I learned how to shell beans and pear in first grade.

Mario Batali

Who was your all-time favorite dinner guest? Author Jim Harrison and friends

Is there an ingredient/food that you always steer clear of? Durian, a Southeast Asian fruit because it has a bad taste and smell.

Would you prefer to cook for one person or 100? For one to ten, so that I can relax and enjoy the meal, too.

How often do you cook at home? Four nights per week, breakfast every day

Do you ever eat junk food or other foods that would surprise us? The occasional Big Mac

Who is your favorite person to cook for? My wife, Susi, and our two sons

What is your favorite city in which to dine? New York City—a constant source of surprise—also Melbourne, Australia

What is your favorite childhood memory involving food? Blackberry picking with the family

Jimmy Bannos

If you could eat only one thing for the rest of your life what would it be? My mother-in-law's homemade braciola with tomato gravy.

Is there an ingredient/food that you always steer clear of? I don't like wild rice—it gets stuck in your teeth.

Did you ever get carried away with hot sauce and make something too hot to eat? When I first started seventeen years ago, I would taste a dish and think it wasn't hot enough, so I'd add some more sauce and it would taste okay to me. However, sometimes it would overpower the customers, and I would have to admit that I did make it too hot. The first huge lesson I learned about cooking with chiles is to take it easy.

Would you prefer to cook for one person or 100? I like to cook for my wife and kids, but I also like cooking at the restaurant because you get the instant gratification and satisfaction of cooking for a crowd of people.

How often do you cook at home? I cook at home more in the summertime when I can grill outside. If I am cooking inside at home and make a mess in the kitchen my wife yells at me, so it's just better to cook outside.

If you weren't a chef what would your occupation would be? Psychoanalyst, which is in a way part of my job even now since I deal with all sorts of different people and personalities and the various issues and problems that come along with running three restaurants.

What is the most romantic dinner you ever cooked? The most romantic dinner I ever had was when my wife cooked for me the first time. She made beef stroganoff, and it was amazing—she's a really great cook.

Do you ever eat junk food or other foods that would surprise us? Pretzels, breadsticks, licorice. I also love a little piece of fried pig fat topped with hot sauce.

Who is your favorite person to cook for? My family

What is your favorite city in which to dine? New Orleans

What is your favorite childhood memory involving food? My best memories are when my mom cooked for me as a child. She made incredible things, everything from Greek style roast chicken with roasted potatoes, to roasted lamb, to egg-lemon soup.

Jorge Rodriguez

What was your worst disaster in the kitchen? A sprinkler system going off on a Saturday night

If you could eat only one thing for the rest of your life what would it be? Rare beef

Would you prefer to cook for one person or 100? The more the better—I love the challenge of putting together more than 100.

How often do you cook at home? Every Monday, but during the summer, I cook at home every weekend.

If you weren't a chef what would your occupation would be? Musician

What is the most romantic dinner you ever cooked? My grandmother's eightieth birthday

Do you ever eat junk food or other foods that would surprise us? Twinkies

What is your most creative/elaborate dish and/or biggest flop? A "celestial" dinner for the pope, while I cooked in Italy

Who is your favorite person to cook for? My children

What is your favorite city in which to dine? New York City

What is your favorite childhood memory involving food? The image of my grandma by the stove twenty hours a day

Gail and Anthony Uglesich

Sam Choy

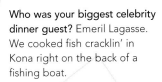

Who was your biggest celebrity dinner guest? Emeril Lagasse. We cooked fish cracklin' in Kona right on the back of a fishing boat.

If you could eat only one thing for the rest of your life what would it be? (Anthony) Any dish that included rice

Is there an ingredient/food that you always steer clear of? Sage—it's too overpowering.

How often do you cook at home? (Gail) I cook every day for the entire family.

If you weren't a chef what would your occupation be? (Anthony) Salesperson—I could sell anything.

Do you ever eat junk food or other foods that would surprise us? (Gail) Yes—potato chips. I could eat an entire bag in one day.

Who is your favorite person to cook for? (Gail) Anthony is my favorite person to cook for because he always has something nice to say.

What is your favorite city in which to dine? (Gail & Anthony) For home cooking—New Orleans; out of state—Las Vegas.

If you could only eat one thing for the rest of your life what would it be? I would need two things—salmon custard and fresh ahi poke.

Would you prefer to cook for one person or 100? It really doesn't matter to me. I just love cooking and can cook for one person or one million people.

How often do you cook at home? About three times a week at home

If you weren't a chef what would your occupation be? Teacher

What is the most romantic dinner you ever cooked? The most romantic dinner I ever cooked was for my wife for our thirtieth wedding anniversary. I made shrimp tempura and an island style teriyaki ribeye for her. For dessert, I made a strawberry shortcake using sponge cake and served it with a scoop of Tahitian vanilla ice cream. I cut the strawberries into little hearts.

Who is your favorite person to cook for? My granddaughter, Tini, is my absolute favorite person to cook for.

What is your favorite city in which to dine? San Francisco and New Orleans

What is your favorite childhood memory involving food? Cooking with my father at the Hawaiian luau they did for 800 people. I remember watching them put the pigs in the imu (underground oven).

Charlie Trotter
Charlie Trotter's
816 West Armitage
Chicago, IL 60614
T: 773.248.6228

www.charlietrotters.com

Emeril Lagasse
Emeril's Restaurant
800 Tchoupitoulas
New Orleans, LA 70130
T: 504.528.9393

Nola Restaurant
542 Rue St. Louis
New Orleans, LA 70130
T: 504.522.6652

Emeril's Delmonico
1300 St. Charles Ave.
New Orleans, LA 70130
T: 504.525.4937

Emeril's N.O. Fish House at
MGM
3799 Las Vegas Blvd. S.
Las Vegas, NV 89109
T: 702.891.7374

Delmonico Steakhouse at the
Venetian
3355 Las Vegas Blvd. S.
Las Vegas, NV 89101
T: 702.414.3737

Emeril's Restaurant, Orlando
6000 Universal Blvd.
Universal Studios CityWalk
Orlando, FL 32819
T: 407.224.2424

www.emerils.com

Lidia Bastianich
Felidia
243 East 58th St.
New York, NY 10022
T: 212.758.1479

Becco
355 West 46th St.
New York, NY 10036
T: 212.397.7597

Lidia's
1400 Smallman St.
Pittsburgh, PA 15222
T: 412.552.0150

Lidia's
101 West 22nd St.
Kansas City, MO
T: 816.221.3722

www.lidiasitaly.com

Daniel Boulud
Café Boulud
20 East 76th St.
New York, NY 10021
T: 212.772.2600

DB Bistro Moderne
44 West 44th St.
New York, NY 10036
T: 212.319.2400

www.danielnyc.com

Marcus Samuelsson
Aquavit
13 West 54th St.
New York, NY 10019
T: 212.307.7311

www.aquavit.org

Rick Bayless
Frontera and Topolobampo
445 North Clark St.
Chicago, IL 60610
T: 312.661.1434

www.fronterakitchens.com

Norman Van Aken
Norman's
21 Almeria Ave.
Coral Gables, FL 33134
T: 305.446.6767

www.normans.com

Sara Moulton
Executive Chef, *Gourmet*
www.gourmet.com

Matthew Kenney
Commissary
1030 Third Ave.
New York, NY 10021
T: 212.339.9955

Commune
2 East 22nd St.
New York, NY 10010
T: 212.777.2600

Commune Atlanta
1198 Howell Mill Rd.
Atlanta, GA 30318
T: 404.609.5000

Commissary Portland
Portland Public Market
25 Preble St.
Portland, ME 04101
T: 207.228.2057

Nickerson Tavern
Main St.
Searsport, ME 04974

Canteen
142 Mercer St.
New York, NY 10012
T: 212.431.7676

Mezze
10 East 44th St.
New York, NY 10017-3601
T: 212.697.6644

Leah Chase
Dooky Chase
2301 Orleans Ave.
New Orleans, LA 70119
T: 504.821.0600

Todd English
Olives
10 City Sq.
Charlestown, MA 02129
T: 617.242.1999

Olives Las Vegas
3600 Las Vegas Blvd. South
Las Vegas, NV 89109
T: 702.693.8181

Olives Washington, DC
World Center Building
1600 K St. NW
Washington, DC 20006
T: 202.452.1866

Olives New York
The W Hotel, Union Square
Park Ave. South
New York, NY 10012
T: 212.353.8345

Figs
67 Main St.
Charlestown, MA 02129
T: 617.242.2229

42 Charles St.
Boston, MA 02114
T: 617.742.3447

92 Central St.
Wellesley, MA 02181
T: 781.237.5788

1208 Boylston St.
Chestnut Hill, MA 02167
T: 617.738.9992

La Guardia Airport
Central Terminal Building
Flushing, NY 11371
T: 718.446.7600

Greg Norman's
4930 Highway 17 South
N. Myrtle Beach, SC 29582
T: 843.361.0000

Olives Aspen
St. Regis Hotel
315 East Deen St.
Aspen, CO 81611
T: 970.920.3300

King Fish Hall
188 Faneuil Hall Marketplace
South Market Building
Boston, MA 02109
T: 617.523.8862

Todd English Rustic Kitchen
200 Quincy Market Building
Faneuil Hall Marketplace,
South East
Boston, MA 02109
T: 617.523.6334

Bonfire
The Boston Park Plaza Hotel
50 Park Plaza
Boston, MA 02116
T: 617.262.3473

Todd English Tuscany
1 Mohegan Sun
Uncasville, CT 06382
T: 860.862.3238

Bobby Flay
Mesa Grill
102 5th Ave.
New York, NY 10011
T: 212.807.7400

Bolo
23 East 22nd St.
New York, NY 10010
T: 212.228.2200

www.mesagrill.com
www.bolorestaurant.com

Bernard Carmouche
Emeril's Restaurant, Orlando
6000 Universal Blvd.
Universal Studios CityWalk
Orlando, FL 32819
T: 407.224.2424

Allan Vernon
Vernon's New Jerk House
987 East 233rd St.
Bronx, NY 10466
T: 718.655.8348

Michael Lomonaco
Noche
1604 Broadway
New York, NY 10019
T: 212.541.7070

Lomonaco's opening in 2003

Mario Batali
Babbo
110 Waverly Pl.
New York, NY 10011
T: 212.777.0303

Lupa
170 Thompson St
New York, NY 10012
T: 212.982.5089

www.babbonyc.com

Jimmy Bannos
Heaven on Seven
111 N. Wabash, 7th Floor
Chicago, IL 60602
T: 312.263.6443

Heaven on Seven on Rush
600 N. Michigan Ave.
Chicago, IL 60611
T: 312.280.7774

Heaven on Seven on Clark
3478 N. Clark St.
Chicago, IL 60657
T: 773.477.7818

www.heavenonseven.com

Jorge Rodriguez
Chimichurri Grill
606 Ninth Ave.
New York, NY 10036
T: 212.586.8655

Gail and Anthony Uglesich
Uglesich's
1238 Baronne St.
New Orleans, LA 70113
T: 504.523.8571

Sam Choy
Sam Choy's Diamond Head
Restaurant
449 Kapahulu Ave., 2nd Floor
Honolulu, HI 96815
T: 808.732.8645

Sam Choy's Breakfast, Lunch,
Crab & Big Aloha Brewery
580 N. Nimitz Highway
Honolulu, HI 96817
T: 808.545.7979

Sam Choy's Kaloko
73-5576 Kauhola St.
Kailua-Kona, HI 96740
T: 808.326.1545

Sam Choy's Guam
1245 Pale San Vitores, Suite 450
Tumon, Guam 96911
T: 671.649.6637

www.samchoy.com